CAREER BUILDING

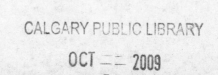

Also by the Editors of CareerBuilder.com

CUBE MONKEYS

CAREER BUILDING

Your Total Handbook for
Finding a Job and
Making It Work

THE EDITORS OF
CareerBuilder.com

COLLINS BUSINESS
An Imprint of HarperCollins Publishers

FIRST EDITION

Designed by Level C

Library of Congress Cataloging-in-Publication Data
Career building: your total handbook for finding a job and making it work/the editors of CareerBuilder.com.
　　p. cm.
Includes bibliographical references and index.
ISBN 978–0–06–157910–3
1. Career development. 2. Job hunting. I. CareerBuilder.com.
HF5381.C2645 2009
650.14—dc22

2008030232

09 10 11 12 13　ov/rrd　10 9 8 7 6 5 4 3 2 1

CONTENTS

INTRODUCTION

Did you know that 84 percent of Americans say they're not in their ideal jobs? Eighty-four percent!

With roughly 153 million people in the U.S. labor force and the average American poised to hold 10.5 jobs in his or her lifetime, one thing's for certain: That's a lot of job dissatisfaction.

To guide you through the sometimes scary world of work, we've compiled this handbook for every step of your career. Why mess with one book for résumés, another for interviewing and still another for salary negotiation? (Not to mention the self-help books you might need once you start your job!) We've got everything right here for you.

The editors of CareerBuilder.com, the United States' largest online job site, have assembled insider tips and tools for any stage of your job search and career. We've divided this book into three sections: job searching, managing your job and co-workers and moving on to the next big thing.

The bottom line: Going to work is a lot of work. But having a successful job search and positive working relationships isn't rocket science. It really comes down to some simple fundamentals. Forget about all that touchy-feely stuff; we're giving work advice straight up. It's tough love. We're not going to tell you to plant a seed and watch it grow . . . sometimes you don't even have time to water it before you know it's rotten!

FINDING "THE ONE"

How many times have you been in this situation? You're at a party making small talk and you're asked, "What do you do for a living?" This is often followed with the obligatory, "Do you like your job?" If the answer is an enthusiastic, "I love it!" chances are you'll be picking the other person up off the floor. That's because most people aren't particularly satisfied with their work situations and would rather be doing something else. This doesn't necessarily mean making a total career change, but finding the right environment, duties and colleagues that fit.

But job searching takes time and work. And, let's face it, it's tough to find the time or energy to focus on a job hunt when you've already got a full plate—your current job, family responsibilities, housework, errands, trying to stay in shape and having some sort of social life.

Whether you've had one job or thirty (ahem, is that something to brag about?), everyone could use a little help in the job search department. Even if you've never written a résumé before, we'll hold your hand through the process and, before you can say, "Hire me!" we'll have you in your next brilliant career.

What's in it for you? Step-by-step résumé writing, cover letter advice and tips on everything job search related; from learning how to decode bogus job ads, to answering the most wrenching interview questions, to what to wear to make the best impression.

Chapter 1

RÉSUMÉS AND COVER LETTERS

Welcome to the puzzling—and often frustrating—world of résumés and cover letters. These are your first chances to make a positive, lasting impression and therefore need to be done right. We're not saying there's a "one size fits all" strategy, but we'll guide you through portraying your best professional self. Apply these steps to your résumé and cover letter writing and put them to the test. If you still don't see results, go back, review some of these sections, and start making some small adjustments. Eventually, you'll get to the right combination. When you notice employers are calling more often and you're getting more interviews, you'll know you're there.

I. WRITING YOUR RÉSUMÉ

STEP ONE: THE FORMULA

Hiring managers spend an average of one minute scanning a résumé. You have just a short window of opportunity to convince them that you're either fabulous or the most boring person alive. Which is it gonna be?

Here are the elements that your résumé should include:

CONTACT INFORMATION: Your name (if your formal name is Abigail, but you go by Abby, use Abby), address, phone number, e-mail address and Web site. Make sure to use a professional e-mail address for your job applications. Employers aren't likely to call HotPants1234@hotmail.com.

CAREER SUMMARY OR OBJECTIVE: These give the hiring manager an idea of who you are immediately—before spending the 60 seconds skimming your résumé and deciding whether to bring you in for an interview. Many job seekers equate a summary with an objective. While both are two to three sentences appearing at the top of your résumé, in reality, they are very different.

An objective states a job seeker's desired job description, and is often ideal for people who are just starting out in the workforce or changing industries. Some words of warning: It could pigeonhole you and limit how employers see you.

Consider this objective:

"Recent college graduate with a bachelor's degree in finance and honors distinction seeks entry-level position in the accounting industry."

If you are looking to take the next step in your chosen field, consider writing a career summary instead. A career summary gives an overview of your work experience and/or relevant education.

This is a career summary:

"Marketing professional with more than ten years experience in online, interactive marketing and advertising in a B2B capacity."

Is there an exception to these rules? Of course. It's not necessary to always include a career summary or an objective, but with hiring managers spending less and less time reviewing résumés, this could give you the edge by summarizing your experience and job goals.

SUMMARY OF QUALIFICATIONS: This calls out the most relevant information for the job. If you include this, the hiring manager doesn't have to hunt for your abilities. This is an easy way to tailor your résumé for each job application. Look at the required skills listed in the job posting and use this as an opportunity to highlight the skills needed for the job. If you are changing careers or industries, this section helps you highlight certain transferable skills.

TECHNICAL SKILLS: This is where you can show your computer and software proficiency. Are you missing a technical skill listed in the job description? Don't throw in the towel. Seventy-eight percent of hiring managers report they are willing to recruit workers who don't have experience in their particular industry or field and provide training/certifications needed.

WORK HISTORY: This is where you list chronologically any work experience—titles, employer and dates of tenure. List only the most recent and *relevant* information; no one cares about your ninth-grade babysitting club . . . unless you are looking for something in childcare (even then, save it for your cover letter).

EDUCATION: Include your dates of graduation, college major and minor, degrees earned or expected graduation date.

STEP TWO: KEYWORDS

You think you have it rough as a job seeker? Hiring managers sort through anywhere from dozens to hundreds of prospective applicants, and some might argue that they have it worse.

Not buying it? We don't blame you—especially because hiring managers have made the job even easier for themselves in recent years. Eager to minimize the task of manually sorting through application after application, employers are increasingly relying on two tools: applicant tracking systems, which scan résumés for key-words relating to skills, training, degrees, job titles and experience, and résumé databases, which employers search for candidates using keywords (similar to how a job seeker searches for a job).

What does this mean for you, the job seeker? The bad news is that a perfectly qualified applicant may never make it as far as an interview merely because his or her résumé lacks certain keywords. The good news is that by finding ways to include these keywords in your résumé, you can gain a strategic advantage over other applicants.

What the . . . ?

So what are these keywords? We're told they're essential to a job search—we should use them in our résumé and cover letter and use them when searching for job openings. But what are they really, and how do you know you're using the right ones? Keywords are specific words or phrases that job seekers use to search for jobs, and employers use to find the right candidates.

Keywords most searched when scanning résumés and cover letters, according to CareerBuilder.com research:

- Problem solving and decision making—53 percent

- Oral and written communications—44 percent

- Leadership—35 percent

- Team building—33 percent

- Performance and productivity improvement—28 percent

- Project management—20 percent

- Customer retention—17 percent

- Strategic planning—13 percent
- Long-range planning—10 percent
- Cost reduction—10 percent
- Business development—10 percent

Other keywords hiring managers may deem important:

- Organizational design
- Internet
- Online
- Digital
- Competitive market
- Product positioning
- MBA
- New media
- E-commerce

DON'T GET LOST IN TRANSLATION. More and more large and medium companies use applicant tracking software. You want to make sure your résumé gets through the gatekeeper by presenting your qualifications as if the reader is comparing the words on the résumé to a list of desired qualifications.

How do you find out the right industry and position-specific buzzwords to use? To understand which keywords and phrases will be most effective for a successful job search, use the following resources:

- **JOB ADS:** Search the job listing of the particular job you're applying for; it will be the best source for keywords that an employer will use. Don't copy the job ad word-for-word, but do borrow some of the language and implement it throughout your résumé. Regurgitating your résumé shows a lack of effort and an employer could dismiss you for doing that. If you're posting a résumé on a job board or industry Web site, search multiple listings and look for the most common buzzwords. Those words have the best chance of being found by the search software.

- **PROFESSIONAL ASSOCIATIONS:** Attend professional association meetings and visit their Web sites, paying attention to industry jargon. Not only will you pick up industry-related terminology that you can use in your résumé, cover letter and during interviews, you will also have a chance to network with other professionals in your field.

- **RECRUITERS OR HEADHUNTERS:** If you're working with a recruiter or headhunter (also called staffing firm), ask for input. Headhunters, whose job it is to know what companies are looking for in a candidate, can tell you which keywords are most relevant to the type of work you're seeking.

- **THE BUREAU OF LABOR STATISTICS (BLS):** The BLS's *Occupational Outlook Handbook* provides information on thousands of jobs and is a great source for job-related keywords.

SO GET KEYED UP. The more keywords you use, the more likely your chances are of getting past a résumé-screening database; however, don't randomly implement keywords just for the sake of having keywords. Your résumé should both make sense to the human who reviews it and be relevant to your own skills and experience. You can also include a keyword summary at the bottom of your résumé. This is simply a list of keywords relevant to your expertise.

Finally, don't stop at your résumé. Utilize keywords in your cover letter, interview and follow-up letter or e-mail, which will indicate that you are knowledgeable about the company and the demands of the job. Make a list of the words you use in your application materials and use those terms when you search online for jobs.

> **BY THE NUMBERS**
> Don't go overboard with keywords. Forty-four percent of employers say they would automatically dismiss a résumé or cover letter that appears to duplicate a job posting.

STEP THREE: LIST YOUR ACCOMPLISHMENTS

Hiring managers told CareerBuilder.com that the most important things in a résumé or cover letter are:

- Relevant experience—73 percent

- Specific accomplishments—46 percent

- Customized to the position—37 percent

- Succinct representation of info—36 percent

- Simple format—25 percent

- Strong objective or career summary—23 percent

- Academic degree—20 percent

Lesson: Vague phrases just don't cut it. This is reason numero uno why you should be constantly updating your résumé. The longer you wait, the more difficult it is to recall the details.

You need to show specific, quantifiable results. Show how you saved your previous employer money, made money for the business, grew the business, cut costs, improved productivity or added clients.

For example:

Instead of, "Effectively managed accounts payable team," write "Managed team of 15 accounts payable specialists and improved productivity by 15 percent with smaller lag time between invoicing and payment."

Write down all the duties for each job on your résumé and then try to add specific numbers to each duty.

SIMPLE RÉSUMÉ TRICK

When was the last time you updated your résumé? Probably not since the last time you looked for a new job, right? Just as you schedule your regular dental appointment, get into the habit of storing information that could be added to your résumé. OK, so actually updating your résumé regularly is somewhat of a long shot. Here's an easy way to keep track of your best accomplishments. Whenever you get the results of a project you worked on, say your monthly sales numbers, send a note about it to your personal e-mail account. Save all these e-mails in a folder marked "résumé" and make the changes quarterly or annually.

Don't forget your soft skills

Yes, we've been pushing the showcasing of accomplishments down your throat, but there's also something to be said about soft skills.

"Soft skills" refer to a cluster of personal qualities, habits, attitudes and social graces that make someone a good employee and compatible co-worker. Companies value soft skills because research suggests and experience shows that they can be just as important an indicator of job performance as hard skills.

Try getting in touch with your soft side. Some of the most common soft skills employers are looking for and will be assessing you on include:

- **STRONG WORK ETHIC:** Are you motivated and dedicated to getting the job done, no matter what? Will you be conscientious and do your best work? Or are you the poster child for slacker? Are you most likely found napping in your car at lunch?

- **POSITIVE ATTITUDE:** Are you optimistic and upbeat? Will you generate good energy and good will? Or are you Debbie Downer?

- **GOOD COMMUNICATION SKILLS:** Are you both verbally articulate and a good listener? Can you make your case and express your needs in a way that builds bridges with colleagues, customers and vendors? Or do you leave people with bewildered looks on their faces?

- **TIME MANAGEMENT ABILITIES:** Do you know how to prioritize tasks and work on many different projects at once? Will you use your time on the job wisely?

- **PROBLEM-SOLVING SKILLS:** Are you resourceful and able to creatively solve problems that will inevitably arise? Will you take ownership of problems or leave them for someone else?

- **ACTING AS A TEAM PLAYER:** Will you work well in groups and teams? Will you be cooperative and take a leadership role when appropriate? Or if things don't go your way will you take your ball and go home?

- **SELF-CONFIDENCE:** Do you truly believe you can do the job? Will you project a sense of calm and inspire confidence in others? Will you have the courage to ask questions that need to be asked and to freely contribute your ideas?

- **ABILITY TO ACCEPT AND LEARN FROM CRITICISM:** Will you be able to handle criticism? Are you coachable and open to learning and growing as a person and as a professional?

- **FLEXIBILITY/ADAPTABILITY:** Are you able to adapt to new situations and challenges? Will you embrace change and be open to new ideas?

- **WORKING WELL UNDER PRESSURE:** Can you handle the stress that accompanies deadlines and crises? Will you be able to do your best work and come through in a pinch?

Focus on the skills most likely to interest the prospective employer and learn to demonstrate these skills through your résumé, in an interview or in dealing with potential employers at career fairs or industry association gatherings.

For example, tell a story of how you successfully handled a crisis or challenge at your company. Mention honors you received or even bring along letters of thanks or commendation from an employer or customer.

TRUE JOB SEEKER STORY
One job applicant brought a legal representative to speak on his behalf at a job interview. Incidentally, he didn't get the job.

STEP FOUR: CHECK FOR MISTAKES

A résumé in and of itself may not get you that killer job, but if you blunder in composing it, you might kill any chance for an interview.

You send a very negative message about your quality of work and attention to detail if your résumé and cover letter contain errors.

Don't rely on your computer's spell-check function. Your computer won't know if you negotiated with unions or onions, or were named manager or manger.

Even if you are a prolific writer, its easy to miss a typo especially after reviewing the document numerous times. After you proofread you résumé a few times, ask someone else to review it. A second pair (or more) of eyes may be able to catch mistakes you missed and could provide a fresh prospective on how to improve your résumé.

Stop! How carefully did you read that last paragraph? If you noticed the three mistakes, you probably wouldn't want to hire us. And if you didn't notice them, get someone to review your résumé stat!

(Errors: "its" in the first sentence should be it's; the second "you" in the second sentence should be your; and "prospective" in the last sentence should be "perspective.")

POP QUIZ: What percentage of hiring managers automatically dismiss résumés or cover letters with spelling or grammatical errors?

A) 25 percent
B) 33 percent
C) 57 percent
D) 66 percent

ANSWER: C. Fifty-seven percent of hiring managers told CareerBuilder.com that résumés and cover letters with errors or typos go straight into the trash bin. Proofread carefully.

Quick fixes to common résumé problems

When it comes to résumés, one size does not fit all. A former supervisor looking for work in a new industry will not have the same résumé as someone who graduated two months ago.

Fortunately, you don't need to panic because you have a circumstance that makes your job hunt a little different than some candidates out there. Here are some quick ways to customize your résumé to your specific needs:

YOU LACK EXPERIENCE: When it comes to the education requirements, you've got that covered. What you're missing is work experience, unless you want to fill your résumé with the details of your childhood paper route and lemonade stand. First, look at the work you've done and highlight the jobs with transferable skills. A retail position probably taught you a lot about customer service and dealing with clients. Also, don't be afraid to include volunteer work, which can display relevant skills and shows your commitment to a cause; 81 percent of employers consider volunteering as work experience. Your involvement in clubs and organizations, such as a fraternity or sorority, can also be important if you held a leadership position. Almost one-third of employers say participation in fraternal organizations qualifies as relevant experience; 19 percent say the same for athletic activities.

YOU'VE HAD A LONG ABSENCE FROM THE WORK FORCE: If you have the experience but have been out of work for a while, your résumé will have a noticeable employment gap. Don't lie by extending the length of employment at your last job because that's information employers can find out in one phone call. Instead, be sure the experience you do have addresses the requirements of the position. Also, mention any refresher courses you took or volunteering you did during your absence. Don't give the hiring manager the chance to wonder whether you're out of touch with current technology or industry practices.

YOUR MOST RECENT JOB LASTED SIX MONTHS: As much as you want a new job to turn into a career you love, it doesn't always work out that way. If you left your last job after only a few months because nothing turned out to be what you expected, think about whether you learned a new skill or refined an old one. The point is to spin the experience into a positive one without bad-mouthing the former employer. Of course, you can leave the job off of the résumé entirely, but expect to be asked about the gap during the interview.

YOU'RE SWITCHING INDUSTRIES: Emphasize your transferable skills. Although your vast knowledge in your current field might go untapped in your new profession, you still possess many skills that will serve you well in your new industry. After all, few people have jobs that directly correlate to their college degree. Why? Because you can learn basic skills and industry information once you begin, but communication and problem-solving skills are assets that serve every job you'll ever have. Focus on what you can bring to the table, not what you lack. Don't list skills that are exclusive to your old industry because they will only make you look too specialized to make a smooth transition.

BY THE NUMBERS

People returning to the work force after an extended absence have an additional concern: Will they even find a job? Yes, they will, according to a CareerBuilder.com survey of employees who have recently returned to the work force. Of surveyed workers who returned to work after being gone at least one year, 45 percent found a job in less than one month. Thirty-three percent took one to six months to find work, while only 14 percent took longer than one year.

Just in case you need a little more help in the résumé department, here's a template you can follow and adjust to your needs.

NAME
Address • City, State ZIP code • E-mail Address • (123) 456–7890

Headline sentence of who you are and what you do. Title with x years experience in x industry/ies, with an understanding and/or experience of x and x. Think of this as your attention-grabbing headline. Be sure to customize this to the keywords of the job you are applying to.

SUMMARY OF QUALIFICATIONS
This is the top ¼ of your résumé, which is the first thing recruiters see. Reading this section should spark their interest. (The rest of your résumé will back up this section.)

Purpose of this section is to summarize your résumé; your relevant key accomplishments, results, actions and benefits.

Try to address each requirement of the job opening in this section. Use the language from the job posting to describe your skills and accomplishments.

Focus on your strong selling points, your value, your achievements, your industry and your career goals.

- Include language proficiencies or security clearances if relevant
- Include education if relevant or recent graduate
- Keep bullets to 1.5 lines max, use only five to eight bullets
- Technical skills
- Certifications, platforms and tools
- List all that are relevant to your current job search

Include technical skills if you are going into an IT/technical position. If not, include your technical skills at the end of your résumé.

PROFESSIONAL EXPERIENCE

TITLE   Month Year–Present
COMPANY   City, State

Short statement of what company does, its functions, its industry, its size (revenue or number of employees).

- First bullet is a quick overview of your responsibilities and duties
- Achievement-focused statements. Quantify, qualify and measure your achievements (use the symbols #, $, %)
- Use numbers ($450,000) instead of words or percentages if number is small
- List achievements in order of importance to job, or list biggest achievements first
- Show how you can solve problems or how the company benefited from you
- Focus on transferable skills and the job you are applying to
- List any awards

TITLE   Month Year–Present

- Use this format for a different title/job at the same company

Make sure to customize your work experience bullets to the job you are applying to. List experience chronologically.

ADDITIONAL EMPLOYMENT

- Title, Company, City, State, Month Year–Month Year
- List jobs here that are not relevant to your current job search or jobs that are over ten years old

EDUCATION AND TRAINING

Degree (BS/BA/etc.)-Emphasis   Year

College/Institution   City, State

     3.7 GPA • Graduation Honor • Honor

SELECTED ACADEMIC PROJECTS *OR*
TRAINING *AND* ACCOMPLISHMENTS

- If you are a recent graduate, list projects that have given you experience
  - List projects, case studies and research that is relevant to the job you are applying for
  - Highlight your ability to solve problems
  - Make sure to focus on your skills, your expertise and what you have achieved
- If you are a professional with work experience, use this section to detail work-related training, conferences, etc.
- Change bullets based on your current job search; make sure most relevant jobs are listed first
- Do not use more than three to four bullets

PROFESSIONAL ASSOCIATIONS AND/OR
TECHNICAL PROGRAMS AND/OR OTHER TITLE

- Member/Office, Organization, City, State, Year–Year
- Award, Year
- Technical programs
- Items in this section should only be included if relevant to your current job search

Do not include irrelevant personal information

Do not say "References provided upon request" or list them

Final notes:

- Make sure to be consistent throughout with bolding, punctuation and phrasing.

- Make sure to proofread, look for typos, grammar mistakes and other errors.

- Make sure it's computer friendly, have two versions—one formatted version for interviews, and another plain text version for Internet correspondence.

- Use Times Roman, Arial or Helvetica 11- or 12-point font.

- Your résumé can be more than one page (this is a myth) but no more than two.

- Make sure to "ignore all" on red and green squiggles or recruiters will see them, too.

- Name your résumé "First Name_Last Name_Resume.doc" (George_Jetson_Resume.doc) not "resume.doc."

- List your contact information on every page.

II. MAKING A GOOD IMPRESSION ON PAPER

What do hiring managers say is their biggest résumé and cover letter pet peeve? Fifty-nine percent say spelling errors.

Here's what else really bugs them:

- Lies—29 percent

- Not customized—23 percent

- Too much detail—20 percent

- Résumé that is longer than two pages—18 percent

- Formatting errors—16 percent

- Irrelevant job experience—15 percent

- Too short, not enough detail—13 percent

- Including the words "references available upon request"—11 percent

> **REASON NO. 1 WHY YOUR PHONE ISN'T RINGING . . .**
> **YOUR RÉSUMÉ AND COVER LETTER ARE AS ARTICULATE AS**
> **FLAVA FLAV'S BLOG.** If your application materials contain typos, grammatical errors and irrelevant or inconsistent information, employers will notice—in a bad way. Once you've looked over your résumé and cover letter to the point of dementia, have three people review your résumé and cover letter before you send them to an employer.

Employers appreciate creative job applicants because rooting through piles of résumés can be monotonous. The key, however, is to balance that creativity with professionalism. You want to stand out as someone unique but also as someone with applicable experience who can add value to the company.

While the goal of a creative résumé is to make a lasting impression, you want to make sure it's a good impression. Here are some things to make sure that happens.

Keep your personal life personal

Hiring managers don't need to know personal information such as your waistline measurement or where you spend your summer vacations. One candidate included that he spent summers on his family's yacht in Grand Cayman, while another included family medical history. Instead, include information on activities that are business-related, such as memberships in professional organizations and community service involvement.

You don't have to share personal information, so be careful when you do. If you do mention something personal, it's fair game in discussions. You might run into someone's bias, so avoid hitting those hot buttons. If you were president of the Young Republicans, your Democrat interviewer may not be impressed, or vice versa. Working for environmental or political causes won't impress everyone the same way. If you list golf as a hobby, someone might think you would spend too much time on the course. Even mentioning leadership roles at your place of worship could keep you from getting an interview.

Listing personal information such as height, weight and age and providing photographs can be a pet peeve. If these points of information don't pertain to the job in question, there's no need to include them. These items—unless you're applying for a modeling job—are not needed and could cause bias on the employer's side.

You can always discuss what's important to you once you are seated face-to-face, but don't deny yourself that opportunity. On the other hand, if you do think something in your personal life *influenced* someone's decision in not hiring you, that's a whole other ball game.

Lose the bling

Remember that scene in *Legally Blonde* when Elle Woods gives her professor a pink scented résumé? Even if you didn't see the movie, the idea alone should set off a red flag. Some people believe that their résumés will stand out in the crowd if they stray from the conventional layout. This might work well if you are sending a résumé for a creative job, like a graphic artist, art director or interior designer, and you know that someone is definitely going to look at it. Or, it could work against you.

For a printed résumé or one you plan to e-mail as an attachment, stay away from the cutesy-pie layouts and formatting. Using a pale blue background with teddy bears around the border (like one candidate did) isn't going to strike anyone as anything but weird. Three key ideas to keep in mind when formatting your résumé: simple, bold and professional. Instead of flashy formatting and stationery with borders or graphics, create a clean and polished document on résumé paper with consistent formatting for headings and bullet points. To gain a hiring manager's attention, use strong action words such as "achieved" and "managed" instead of unconventional fonts or colored text.

TRUE RÉSUMÉ BLUNDERS

You've used all your creative juices to build a résumé that stands out in the crowd—but have you gone overboard? Hiring managers and human resources professionals nationwide shared the most unusual résumé blunders they came across:

- Candidate included a picture of herself in a cheerleading uniform.
- Candidate attached a letter from her mother.
- Candidate declared that he worked well nude.
- Candidate explained a gap in employment by saying it was because he was getting over the death of his cat for three months.
- Candidate specified that his availability was limited because Friday, Saturday and Sunday was "drinking time."

Keep outdated info out

We said it once, we'll say it again: Leave off the activities that you did in high school if graduation was a few years ago, and omit jobs you held ten or more years ago. The information is probably irrelevant to the position you're trying for now.

One size does NOT fit all

If you're applying for a sales position, it wouldn't make much sense to focus on your experience in an unrelated field like education or information technology. Not only should you play up achievements and experience specific to the job you're applying for, but also provide quantifiable results. For example, it's easy to say that you have experience in sales, but employers will take note if you say that you were responsible for a 10 percent growth in overall sales.

No giving yourself a "promotion"

Augmenting your credentials with a little fiction might help you get the job, but you almost certainly will be found out. Although just 5 percent of workers admit to fibbing on their résumés, 57 percent of hiring managers say they have caught a lie on a candidate's application, according to data from CareerBuilder.com. Of those hiring managers who caught a lie, 93 percent did not hire the candidate.

This could also cause termination sometime down the road. Worse, you will have gravely harmed your reputation within your chosen industry. Industry people travel in the same circles. It's highly likely that your employer will someday bump into someone who knows the real you, so don't say you were Phi Beta Kappa if you were a C student. Even a little white lie can backfire.

Mind the gaps

While you want to forget that time you were unemployed for a year, you really should account for gaps in employment. But be careful with your wording. "One of the weirdest things that I ever saw on a résumé . . . was a candidate who explained a ten-year lapse in work experience as being in jail during those years for killing her husband," recalls one recruiting manager. In such a situation, the best thing to write would be "left work for personal reasons," and the candidate would be able to explain the criminal record later.

> **REASON NO. 2 WHY YOUR PHONE ISN'T RINGING . . . YOU MISREPRESENT YOURSELF.** It may sound like a no-brainer, but misrepresenting yourself on a résumé is bound to catch up with you. Upon performing a reference check, one hiring manager told us she discovered a job candidate had left her previous job one year earlier than she'd admitted. It turned out that the candidate had gotten burned out and decided to take a year to temp and regroup, but thought the obvious employment gap would be held against her, so she simply lied about it. "I figured if she'd lie about something this easy to explain, she might lie about the deadline-driven work she would have to do with me," she said.

III. FIVE STEPS TO AN E-FRIENDLY RÉSUMÉ

In case you haven't noticed, we've entered the twenty-first century—in fact, we've been here for quite some time.

Now that you've written your résumé, you need to make sure it's compatible with today's Internet-driven world. Gone are the days of handwritten cover letters, typewriter-printed résumés and hand-delivered job applications. Given the increase in online job boards that require Web-based applications, many employers don't want a hard copy of your résumé. Instead, they'll ask you to submit an electronic résumé, either online or via e-mail. In fact, a digital résumé is the main contact medium for 70 percent of U.S. employers.

Electronic résumés are plain text or HTML documents, which can also be included in the body of an e-mail for job applications online. It may not be as attractive as your Word-formatted résumé in all its bulleted, bold-text, fancy-font glory; but it gets the job done.

WHY YOU NEED ONE

When an employer asks you to submit your application materials via e-mail or online, it's likely that he or she will enter your résumé into an automated applicant-tracking system or ATS. Unfortunately, these systems don't care what your résumé looks like physically, which is why it's imperative you reformat yours so the database can read it. The system will scan your résumé (along with hundreds of others), keeping those with keywords similar to their job descriptions and discarding the rest.

However, make sure you keep a hard (and visually appealing) copy of your résumé on hand—not all employers are up-to-date on the latest technologies. Some may still require a paper résumé or one e-mailed as an attachment. Plus, you'll also need it to print out and give to employers at all of those interviews you score.

You can remove the formatting and still have it be easy to read. Here are five easy steps to format your existing résumé into an e-friendly work of art:

1. Remove all formatting from your original résumé

Unfortunately, the same formatting that makes your résumé nice to look at makes it virtually impossible for a computer to understand.

Open your word-processed résumé and choose the "Save As" option under the File tab on your toolbar. Save the document type as Plain Text or Text Only. In the following dialogue box, choose the option to insert line breaks.

2. Use Notepad, WordPad or SimpleText to reformat

Close your original résumé document and re-open the text version using Notepad, WordPad or SimpleText software. This will remove any formatting that could look weird if not compatible with someone else's software.

You'll notice that your text version is—at least it should be—free of most graphic elements, like elaborate fonts, lines or bullets. Text should be flush with the left side of the document.

3. Stick to a simple font and style

Use clear, sans-serif fonts, like Courier, Arial or Helvetica. This way, the computer won't mistake your fancy lettering for a jumbled word.

Use a 12-point font; anything smaller won't scan well. Also, stay away from italics or underlining. Rather than using boldface type, try using capital letters to separate sections like education and experience.

Instead of using bullets, use typical keyboard characters like an asterisk or a dash. As an alternative to using the Tab key to indent, use the space bar.

Make sure all headings—like your name, address, phone and

e-mail—all appear on separate lines, with a blank line before and after.

4. Apply keywords

Applicant tracking systems scan résumés for keywords that match the company's job descriptions. Fill your résumé accordingly with such words (as they pertain to your experience), but remember that using the same word five times won't increase your chances of getting called in for an interview. Try to use nouns rather than action verbs.

For example: "communications specialist," "sales representative" or "computer proficiency" are better than "managed," "developed" or "generated."

Place the most important words first, since the scanner may be limited in the number of words it reads. Additionally, avoid abbreviations as best you can. Spell out phrases like, "bachelor of science" or "master of business administration."

5. Test it out

After you've reformatted your résumé into a seemingly boring text document, make sure it really is e-friendly. Practice sending your e-résumé via e-mail to yourself, as well as friends who use different Internet service providers. For example, if you use AOL, send it to a friend who uses MSN Hotmail.

Send your e-résumé pasted in the body of an e-mail, rather than as an attachment. Have your friends alert you of any errors that appear when they open it, like illegibility, organization, etc. After getting their feedback, make any necessary adjustments.

Welcome to the twenty-first century!

POP QUIZ: What is the most effective way to e-mail a résumé to a potential employer?

A) Copy and paste it into the body of the e-mail
B) Attach it as a plain text file
C) Attach it as a PDF file
D) Attach it as a Word document

ANSWER: A. Sending an employer a virus that crashes his or her computer will kill your chances of landing the job. Plus, the hiring manager might hesitate to open attachments from unknown senders.

IV. COVER LETTER DOS AND DON'TS

It's the age-old question from job seekers: Must every résumé be accompanied by a cover letter? The answer, according to professional career counselors, is a resounding YES. One-in-five employers will automatically throw your résumé in the recycling bin if you don't have a cover letter to go with it, according to a CareerBuilder.com survey.

And not just any cover letter. It must be tailored to the specific job to which you are applying. Experts say that it takes just seven seconds to make a first impression. If a hiring manager sees you don't have a cover letter upon first perusing your application, it's possible you could lose all chances of being contacted for that job.

In an extremely competitive job market, neglecting your cover letter is a big mistake. It's your first opportunity to tell a prospective employer about yourself and to do so in your own words. Like a written interview, a cover letter gives you the opportunity to point out applicable experience and qualities that make you right for the job. And just like any other important job searching tool, there are definite dos and don'ts to follow to make sure your cover letter is an asset, not a hindrance.

REASON NO. 3 WHY YOUR PHONE ISN'T RINGING . . .
**YOUR LETTER IS A CLIFF'S NOTES VERSION OF YOUR
RÉSUMÉ.** Instead of simply restating what's on your résumé,
include new information such as how you found out about the
job, why you want to work there and what you can do for them.
Finally, close with something that will encourage a response,
such as a request for an interview.

Here are some tips for a foolproof cover letter:

COVER THE BASICS

The majority of hiring managers say a cover letter should be two
to three paragraphs. Your letter should be brief, easy to read and
always include your full name, address and phone number, in case
your cover letter becomes separated from your résumé. Hiring
managers receive letters and résumés from dozens, even hundreds
of applicants, and often just don't have the time to read lengthy,
wordy letters. Be direct. In the first paragraph, include the title of
the position you are interested in and then move on to your specific
qualifications immediately.

TARGET IT

You expect the company to take the time to read through your
material, so you too need to take some time to research the correct
addressee. Cover letters that begin with phrases like "To Whom It
May Concern," sound like random junk or bulk mail, rather than
an important correspondence. Avoid using "Dear Hiring Manager"
and find out the name of the human resources contact or recruiter.
You can find this information by logging on to the company's Web
site or calling the main phone number and asking a receptionist for
the name and title of their corporate recruiter.

GET IN THEIR FACES

You need to grab your reader's attention immediately. What's the effect you want to have? Try aiming for something just short of smacking someone upside the head; one-third of hiring managers won't read on if you don't capture their attention in the first sentence. Additionally, watch the cheese factor; you don't want to go overboard.

Instead of: "I read with great interest the job available at your impressive company." Try: "You're seeking a creative thinker with stellar writing skills and media relations experience. That person is me."

BE DETAILED

State which job you are applying for in the very first paragraph. Make sure to include other specific details such as a job ID number (if one was provided) and where you heard about the opening. The reason for this detail is simple: Many recruiters are responsible for multiple openings within their companies and must be able to determine which job your application is targeting. If an employee referred you for the position, be sure to mention that person in your letter, as many companies have employee referral programs.

Show the hiring manager that you paid attention. If a company advertises that it is looking for statistical analysis experience, make sure you address your experience in that area in the cover letter. One way to do this is by making a two-column chart for yourself before writing your letter. List the company's stated needs in one column, and your corresponding experience and qualifications in another column. You can then use that information to write a letter that tells them exactly what they want to know.

HAVE PERSONALITY

Don't send a generic cover letter. Hiring managers can spot a mass mailing a mile away. One objective of a good cover letter is to make a personal connection with the reader. Gone are the days when you could simply change the name of the company in your salutation, attach it to your résumé and fire it off to the employer. Recruiters see right through these types of letters and recognize them for what they are—a lazy person's attempt to find a job. In fact, almost half said they'd automatically dismiss a candidate whose résumé or cover letter is not customized.

> **REASON NO. 4 WHY YOUR PHONE ISN'T RINGING . . .** **YOUR LETTER EXUDES SELF-CONSCIOUSNESS, NOT SELF-CONFIDENCE.** If you don't feel qualified for a job, why are you applying for it? Don't call attention to your shortcomings in a letter; emphasize your strengths by focusing on your skills, experience and ability.

DO SOME LEGWORK

A winning cover letter will require some research into the company's history and recent accomplishments. It should show the reader that you have some knowledge of the company and that you made an informed decision when you decided to apply for the job. What gets attention are letters that address the company—and its needs—specifically. Research the company prior to writing the letter. Check out recent news and read the company's Web site, and then incorporate what you learned into your letter. Doing so will demonstrate to employers that you are informed, motivated and willing to go the extra mile.

SHOW YOUR WORTH

Remember, it's not what the company can do for you; it's what you can do for the company. Don't make the reader work too hard to see that you are right for the position. When writing your letter, keep the requirements of the job in mind and address them specifically. Include specific examples about your past successes and experience. If you are looking for a marketing position, give the reader detailed information about a marketing campaign you successfully executed. Don't just tell the reader that you are motivated; give an example that shows your motivation. Show the person making the hiring decision how your experience and qualities fit the company's needs.

GET THE INTERVIEW

Nobody gets a job by sitting at home waiting for the phone to ring. Don't end your letter passively. Go ahead and tell the hiring manager you want that interview (without arrogance). Express that your cover letter and résumé are just the tip of the iceberg and you look forward to a face-to-face conversation. Similarly, not many people get a call once a résumé or cover letter is sent. Since you are the one looking for work, you need to take the initiative and follow up. Instead of ending the letter with "I look forward to hearing from you," close with "I will call or e-mail you next week to discuss a time for us to meet." Once you've included this call to action, however, make sure you follow up on your own promise.

CHECK IT TWICE

Don't forget to proofread your letter with great care. Nothing says "I don't really want this job" like a cover letter with typos, incorrect information or spelling errors. Make sure the job title and employer name are correct, too. And, while it sounds almost too obvious to mention, be sure to sign your letter. Careless—and easily correctable—mistakes tell the company that you did not take this simple task seriously.

> **REASON NO. 5 WHY YOUR PHONE ISN'T RINGING . . . YOU CROSS THE LINE FROM SOUNDING CONFIDENT TO SOUNDING COCKY.** Don't mistake selling yourself with bragging. Putting "I would be an asset to your company" in your cover letter catches the eye; writing "You would be crazy not to hire me" turns the stomach.

Cover Letters: Do this. . .

Eric A. Marks
3140 Meadow Brook
Chicago, IL 60601
(312) 555–5555
ericmarks@emails.com

Isabelle Brandon, Chief Marketing Coordinator
Bradley Studios
1000 Oceanside Avenue #823
Chicago, IL 60601
(312) 555–5555

Dear Ms. Brandon:

Bradley Studios' reputation as the premier fashion retailer with innovative in-store designs compelled me to apply for the visual coordinator position. I have the artistic background, creative ideas and communication skills that are in line with your cutting-edge work and can deliver new and exciting concepts.

As an intern at Jones Graphics, I assisted with several marketing efforts, including the successful Goldman & Heart Clothiers ad campaign, which won three industry awards, garnered media attention, and increased the company's visibility. During my two years with the company I offered my thoughts and ideas, many of which were incorporated into the campaigns. I also learned a great deal from working next to Clyde Harvey, who was a fantastic mentor and recommended this position to me because of his wonderful history with you during his time at Bradley Studios.

My educational background in studio art and communications allows me to bring a creative eye to any task I take on while keeping in mind the importance of accurately communicating the message to customers. I understand that the best ideas need to be original and attention-grabbing without alienating clients.

I have long admired the artistic integrity of Bradley Studios and believe I can uphold your high standards. I look forward to meeting you in an interview.

Sincerely,

Eric Marks

Eric A. Marks

Not this. . .

Marianne Ross
658 January Drive
Chicago, IL 60601
(312) 555–5555
DrunkDiva@emails.com

August 1, 2009

Anderson Supplies, Inc.
5113 Carolina Street
Chicago, IL 60601

To Whom It May Concern:

 I read your job posting on CareerBuilder.com and am writing in response to the ad you posted for the Sales Supervisor at Midwest Electrical. I am looking for a position that will further my career in sales.

 As you can see from my enclosed résumé, I have the skills and experience to be successful in this position.

 Regarding salary, I expect to earn $75,000 and have full benafits and at least three weeks of vacation time.

 I look forward to hearing from you in the future.

      Sincerely,
      Marianne Ross

Chapter 2

FINDING THE JOBS

Now that your résumé is ready for its debut, it's time to put it to the test. You need to actually start applying to jobs—jobs you are truly suited for. (Employers are constantly baffled by applicants who have no expertise for the job and show no transferable skills.) This means finding jobs that meet your skill set as well as fit you as a person.

I. WHERE TO SEARCH

You should approach job hunting just as you would finding a birthday present: Shop and compare 'til you find the perfect one. To find the most jobs that are right for you, you need to cast the widest net possible and use every resource available to you. Use only one way to search or one job board, and your chances of finding a job are severely impaired.

Here are places to look:

ONLINE RECRUITMENT SITES: Of course we're going to toot our own horn and tell you to use CareerBuilder.com. But we wouldn't be giving you the best advice if we didn't tell you to use every resource you can find: Look at other job boards, from ours to the smallest niche sites. Sign up with several and register to receive e-mail updates.

COMPANY WEB SITES: Look at business publications and see which companies are lauded for high growth, happy employees and best business practices. Keep a list of any companies that stand out to you. Search online for a company's Web site and see if it has an employment section. If the Web site doesn't feature available jobs, call the human resources department and inquire if there are any openings for which you are qualified.

INDUSTRY ASSOCIATIONS: Check out the Web sites of professional organizations related to your job or industry. Most have job listings. Attend an event in your area and get to know your peers. You'll be able to make personal connections, do some marketing for yourself and possibly hear about positions that aren't even advertised.

WORD OF MOUTH: Just like it works for Kevin Bacon, so can six degrees of separation work for you. Tell your friends and family that you are in the market for a new job. It could be they know of a position directly or they are connected to someone who knows of a position.

> **REASON NO. 6 WHY YOUR PHONE ISN'T RINGING . . .**
> **YOU ASSUME E-MAIL IS ENOUGH.** Hitting the Send button on an online application is only the first step in landing an interview. For one thing, not every e-mail is received or read. Try following up your application by sending a paper résumé and cover letter via snail mail (indicating you've already applied online). After that, call the hiring manager to see that your application was received and check on the status of the job in question.

II. SEARCH ONLINE WITH KEYWORDS

You run searches on everything else, from your high school sweetheart to low-fat recipes, so why not jobs? Enter a query that describes the exact kind of job you're seeking and you may find more resources you wouldn't find otherwise (but be prepared to do some sorting).

Go back to that list of keywords you wrote in Chapter 1. You can use them as search criteria on a job board in the same way you do research on the Internet. The more keywords you use, the more closely the job will match your expertise. For example, if you type the word "retail" into a search engine, you'll get literally thousands of job descriptions. But if you type the phrase "merchandising manager," you're going to get fewer, more useful results.

III. CRACKING THE JOB LISTING CODE

If you've ever looked at a job listing and thought, "I'd be perfect for this job, if only . . . ," you understand the discouragement a lot of job seekers feel.

When it comes to meeting the qualifications for a job, is there any flexibility? That depends on the employer, but in most cases, the answer is yes. Certainly, it helps to understand how your own experience and needs match up to what the employer wants and is willing to offer, which isn't always an easy task, thanks to the obscure language typical of many job listings.

Here are some common job listing terms and what they really mean for job candidates.

"Preferred skills" and "Required skills"

When a job listing says "required," that's a requirement that is of the utmost importance to the hiring manager. A skill that's listed as "preferred" is not necessarily essential for a candidate to have.

In today's competitive world, however, it's unrealistic for employers to expect to get a candidate who meets all of their requirements, and employers may relax some of those requirements for a candidate who meets at least most of the requirements.

"Command of" and "Working knowledge of"

If you have "working knowledge of" a certain program, you know the basics of how to operate that program; if you have "command of" a program, you have enough experience with it to be able to explain how it works and use it for more complex projects or a higher level of work.

"Entry Level" and "Experienced"

If a job posting indicates it's an entry-level position, employers are typically looking for someone who has been out of college up to two years. "Experienced" candidates usually have been working for three or more years in the industry or have graduate degrees, which can account for some work experience.

Salary requirements

Confused by terms like "competitive" or "scale"? When it comes to salary, research is essential. Online salary sites like CBsalary.com provide the average pay for one's profession, city and level of experience. By figuring out what the "competitive" salary for that job is, candidates can figure out their worth and put up an asking price that's fair to both themselves and employers.

If an employer asks for salary requirements, you should try to avoid it altogether, because if you name a salary that's too low, you are selling yourself short; but if you give too high a number, you can automatically take yourself out of the running. The best way to avoid providing a requirement is to give a range—one that you can live with. Again, do your research beforehand.

There's less wiggle room, however, when employers ask job seekers to provide salary histories. Because employers can easily verify a candidate's history, it's best to be up front about that.

If you're still unsure as to whether your skills match a certain job or whether you'd fit in with a company, get an inside opinion. Try to network within the company or the industry to meet people who can answer your questions or advise you.

> **REASON NO. 7 WHY YOUR PHONE ISN'T RINGING . . .**
> **YOU GIVE UP.** Remember that looking for work is a full-time job. If you're not hearing back from employers, consider changing your strategy. Experiment with different cover letters, revise your résumé regularly and look for opportunities to add to your experience even when you're not working (i.e., taking classes, participating in workshops, volunteering).

IV. PROTECTING YOURSELF FROM SCAMS

Anyone who has ever looked for a job has certainly seen countless ads that sound unbelievably awesome. They probably included phrases such as:

Make $4,000 a Week from Home—No Sales!
No experience necessary!
Earn $35,000—$50,000 a year working part-time!

Sounds great, right? Well, like most things in life, if it seems too good to be true, it usually is.

From envelope-stuffing schemes to mystery-shopper promotions, the world of scam ads is wide and complex. The problem with many work-at-home schemes is that they require the worker to spend their own money to get started and, once they do, there's often no return on investment. In many cases, you will have to foot the bill for supplies, starter kits, training and more. Other situations that claim to be "easy money with no sales" often do involve a great deal of sales work in challenging environments.

While there are credible work-at-home opportunities out there, many of these ads are not the real thing. The clues listed below can help you figure out if an ad is a great opportunity or a dangerous scam.

First, make yourself aware of the most common scams surrounding the online job industry. Second, be aware of indications that a job might be fraudulent. Last but not least, know who to reference when you need help determining a job's or employer's legitimacy.

Signs of a scam

When searching for a job online, there are several things you should look out for.

- As a job seeker, the best prevention is to avoid being tempted by offers that appear to be "too good to be true."

- Be cautious of any employer offering employment without an interview, either by phone or in person. No legitimate employer will hire you without first conducting an interview.

- Thoroughly investigate any employer who requires some type of payment before you can start working for them. Rarely will you find a legitimate employer requesting a fee . . . they should be paying you!

- Do not provide copies of your driver's license, passport, Social Security card or any other sensitive information unless you are confident that the employer requesting the information is legitimate. Identity thieves thrive on this info.

- Avoid vague offers, as these are often scams. If the employer is not willing to specifically describe the position, you probably don't want it.

- Do not give out personal financial information such as checking, savings, credit card or PayPal account numbers.

- Phrases like "package forwarding," "reshipping," "money transfer," "wiring funds" and "foreign agent agreements" are red flags.

What you can do . . .

Even armed with this knowledge, you may still find yourself questioning a job you found online. Luckily there are still options available to you.

SEARCH ENGINES: Try entering the company name into any search engine—like Google, Ask or Yahoo!—and review the results. Not surprisingly, searches on the popular search engines also offer pertinent information when trying to determine the legitimacy of an offer.

THE SOURCE OF THE JOB: If the job was found on a job board, report it to customer service.

THE BETTER BUSINESS BUREAU: This consumer advocacy organization allows you to search its database of customer inquiries and complaints about a certain company.

Web site: http://www.bbb.org/.

FEDERAL TRADE COMMISSION: If consumers have concerns about a company's advertisements for employment services, they should contact the FTC's Consumer Response Center, toll-free, at 1–877–382–4357.

Web site: www.ftc.gov.

LAW ENFORCEMENT: File a report online with the FBI Internet Crimes division. You may also want to contact your local authorities to make them aware of the situation.

Web site: www.ic3.gov

> **REASON NO. 8 WHY YOUR PHONE ISN'T RINGING . . .**
> **YOU ASSUME THE INTERNET IS ENOUGH.** The majority of all employment opportunities aren't advertised, so be proactive: Contact human resources managers at companies you want to work for to inquire about available positions; register with a job recruitment agency; attend industry events to stay on top of news and devote energy to meeting like-minded professionals who will be the keys to discovering more opportunities.

V. USING A STAFFING FIRM OR A RECRUITER

Plenty of people will tell you that job hunting is full-time work. They're right. Not only do you have to scour job postings, you also have to send out countless résumés and go on several interviews—not to mention the high stress level that comes with a job change. For these very reasons, job seekers go to recruiters or staffing firms who search for you.

How to pick the right one

Sure, it sounds like obvious and easy advice, but picking the right recruiter can make the difference between finding the perfect job match and going on endless interviews for positions you don't want.

First, you need to decide if you want a recruiter who matches clients with jobs in all industries or one who focuses only on one industry, also known as a niche recruiter. If you're looking to branch out into a new industry or career path, however, a general recruiter might be a better fit.

To find the right recruiter or staffing firm, try the following:

- Ask your colleagues which recruiters they have used and recommend.

- Look for advertisements in trade magazines about the industry in which you're interested.

- When you're contacted by headhunters or you see job postings that interest you, even when you're not looking for a job, write down the contact information for later use.

- The Internet can lead you in the right direction as long as you know what you want.

Make the most of your recruiting experience

Recruiters can ease your stress level and workload, but you still need to put forth some effort to make your job hunt successful.

Be honest

Recruiters aren't mind readers. They can only find the right job if they know what you're looking for, so be forthcoming about what you want. In addition to telling your recruiter about your salary requirements and your ideal job description, explain what personalities you'd like to see in your co-workers and the type of office culture you prefer. Give the recruiter as many details as possible about your desires and reasons for switching jobs.

Give feedback

When your recruiter sets up interviews for you, give feedback afterward. Recruiters want to know how things went and if the job was what you were looking for. Feedback helps them understand if they're leading you down the right path or if they need to change direction.

Keep your recruiter in the loop

Full disclosure is also important when dealing with your recruiter. He or she needs to know if you know somebody at the company, if you've already applied for a position in the past or if another recruiter has contacted the company on your behalf.

Have patience

Before getting a recruiter, you probably looked for jobs yourself, so you know it's a time-consuming process. Keep that in mind when waiting to hear back from your recruiter.

Make sure your recruiter is working for you

Although you need to be patient and your recruiter gets paid by the hiring company to find the perfect candidate for the job, you want to know he or she hasn't forgotten you. If you never hear back from your recruiter about any interviews, take that as a sign you should find someone else.

BY THE NUMBERS

When looking at the usage levels for 2007, more than one-in-three employers (37 percent) used at least one staffing firm/recruiter to find qualified candidates, and nearly one-in-four employers (23 percent) used at least two. More than one-in-ten employers (12 percent) used three or more staffing firms/recruiters in 2007.

Chapter 3

THE INTERNET VS. YOUR PROFESSIONAL IMAGE

Great parties usually mean great pictures, but think long and hard before uploading those photos to your social networking Web page. The proliferation of social networking sites and powerful search engines makes it easy for friends to keep track of you, but friends aren't the only ones who will have access to your latest escapades. Don't fret, you can take control of your online image so the Internet works for, not against, you.

I. WHAT'S HAPPENING ON THE EMPLOYER END

That cute, affable guy who brags of his drunken exploits on Facebook may be meeting a lot of other partiers online, but he's probably not getting added to the "friends" lists of many corporate recruiters.

You'd be surprised at what recruiters have seen when researching candidates online. From risqué photos to racial slurs and lewd comments, they've seen it all.

As the amount of personal information available online grows, first impressions can be formed long before the interview process begins. Given the implications and the shelf-life of Internet content, managing your online image is something everyone should address—regardless of whether you're in a job search.

You need to know employers can be privy to information you might not want them to find. There can be consequences to making your personal life public. According to CareerBuilder.com research, 22 percent of employers report they use social networking sites to research job candidates.

Many of these employers don't like what they find. In 2008, of the managers who browsed social networking sites, 34 percent found dirt that caused them to dismiss a candidate.

REASON NO. 9 WHY YOUR PHONE ISN'T RINGING . . .
YOUR MYSPACE PAGE LISTS "BINGE-DRINKING" AS A FAVOR-ITE PASTIME. Don't post anything on a publicly accessible Web site that you wouldn't want a potential employer to see. Not all hiring managers run searches on job candidates, but some do, and it's better to err on the side of caution. Search online using your name to see what comes up, because recruiters will see the same results.

Interestingly, many candidates are far more honest online than they are on their résumés. Twenty-seven percent of hiring managers say they have disqualified a candidate after discovering the candidate had lied about his or her qualifications. Other dismissals resulted from:

- Poor communication skills (29 percent)

- Criminal behavior (21 percent)

- Bad-mouthing previous companies or employees (28 percent)

- Posting information about drinking or drug use (41 percent)

- Disclosing confidential information about previous employers (19 percent)

- Provocative or inappropriate photographs (40 percent)

- Unprofessional screen name (22 percent)
- Discriminatory remarks related to race, gender, religion, etc. (22 percent)

II. YOU'VE GOT A REP TO PROTECT

Not all employers search candidates and employees online, but the trend is growing. Don't let online social networking deep-six your career opportunities. Protect your image by following these simple tips:

BE CAREFUL. Nothing is private. Don't post anything on your site or your friends' sites you wouldn't want a prospective employer to see. Derogatory comments, revealing or risqué photos, foul language and lewd jokes will all be viewed as a reflection of your character.

BE DISCREET. If your network offers the option, consider setting your profile to "private," so that it is viewable only by friends of your choosing. And since you can't control what other people say on your site, you may want to use the "block comments" feature. Remember, everything on the Internet is archived, and there is no eraser!

BE PREPARED. Check your profile regularly to see what comments have been posted. Use a search engine to look for online records of yourself to see what is out there about you. If you find information you feel could be detrimental to your candidacy or career, see about getting it removed—and make sure you have an answer ready to counter or explain "digital dirt."

III. IT'S NOT ALL BAD

While sharing information online can have a potentially negative impact on your job search or career plans, it can also be leveraged as a tool to differentiate yourself to employers. Twenty-four percent of hiring managers said the information discovered on a candidate's social networking page helped to confirm their decision to hire a candidate. Top factors that influenced the decision included:

- Background information that supported the candidate's professional qualifications (48 percent)

- A wide range of interests (30 percent)

- Great communication skills (43 percent)

- A professional image (36 percent)

- Signs that the candidate would be a good personality fit for the company culture (40 percent)

For example, one hiring manager did a search online of one candidate to find out he was on the boards of several philanthropic organizations. Another hiring manager learned of a candidate's public speaking abilities from a video posted online from her college graduation.

IV. DAMAGE CONTROL

So what do you do if you find a blemish on your cyber rep? Not to fear, there are some simple things you can do to clear it up.

If you know the person . . .

Say you've been tagged in a not so flattering photo of you on New Year's Eve that you prefer nobody, especially your mother or new boss, see. If you can, remove the tag yourself. If that doesn't work, ask the person who uploaded the photo to remove it or at least the tag. If that person doesn't comply, you can always report the picture to the site's administrator or get creative with Photoshop and doctor up a not so nice pic of the culprit. (Just kidding on that last one, of course!)

If you don't know the person or site administrator . . .

If there's false information written about you in a social column or alumni newsletter, there are ways to get it corrected, too. Check out the "Contact Us" info, which is usually found either at the bottom or top corner of the home page. Then put in a request for the information to be corrected.

Chapter 4

INTERVIEWS 101 AND BEYOND

So you've rocked your résumé and finessed your cover letter, you got the call and finally have an interview! But now what? The nerves start to kick in, you're anxious and all you can think about is making a great first impression. Wait. Are you job searching or dating?

Think of an interview as a blind date. Going in, you have the highest of expectations: You want to impress the person, you hope that person does the same for you and you hope it's a great match. How you look and act, and what you talk about determine the outcome. It's a two-way street and each person is testing the waters. In this chapter, we're going to tell you how to get from the first date to the second and then, hopefully, to a long-term and loving relationship.

WE'RE NOT JOKING . . .

Some real-life interview jaw droppers, as told to CareerBuilder.com:

- Candidate said there were some days he just couldn't give 100 percent.
- Candidate told the interviewer he wouldn't be able to stay with the job long because he thought he might get an inheritance if his uncle died—and his uncle wasn't "looking too good."
- Candidate asked the interviewer for a ride home after the interview.
- Candidate smelled his armpits on the way to the interview room.
- Candidate said she could not provide a writing sample because all of her writing had been for the CIA and it was "classified."
- Candidate told the interviewer he was fired for beating up his last boss.
- When applicant was offered food before the interview, he declined saying he didn't want to line his stomach with grease before going out drinking.
- A candidate for an accounting position said she was a "people person" not a "numbers person."
- Candidate flushed the toilet while talking to interviewer during phone interview.
- Candidate took out a hairbrush and brushed her hair.
- Candidate inquired about the location of the company's security cameras.
- Candidate admitted she would not pass the mandatory drug test.
- Candidate brought wine to the interview and offered the interviewer a glass.
- Candidate answered his cell phone and asked the interviewer to leave her own office because it was a "private" conversation.

I. INTERVIEW BASICS

It happens all the time: A candidate looks perfect on paper, but once he starts talking in the interview, the hiring manager can't wait to hustle him out the door. Even the most well-prepared, intelligent job seeker can turn into a bumbling mess once anxiety enters the equation. Nerves can't be avoided—but some of the most common interview mistakes can and even the smallest thing can make all the difference.

Timing is everything

Getting to the interview is never as simple as expected. If you need to be there promptly at 8 a.m., you can bet there will be snow, grid-locked traffic or a complete meltdown of your city's public transportation system. Since you can't precisely predict your commute time, leave as early as you can. It may be only five minutes to you, but showing up late for an interview is inappropriate. Do what you have to do to get out the door early. Worst-case scenario: You sit in the parking lot and listen to your iPod until it's time to go in.

Clothes make the (wo)man

If punctuality is important, dressing appropriately is downright crucial. Hiring managers complain that candidates come to interviews dressed in T-shirts, jeans and flip-flops. Research the company dress code and dress one level above company policy. If you find the company dress code is business casual, for example, then plan to wear dress slacks or a skirt and blouse. If the company code is casual, plan to dress at the business casual level—which may mean khakis or other comfortable slacks or skirts paired with proper shirts. If you have any doubt what clothing will be appropriate, wear a suit.

The company does what?

Your preparation shouldn't stop with your wardrobe. Never walk into an interview without at least a working knowledge of the company, its products and its industry. An interviewer will often ask, "What do you know about our business, firm, company, etc.?" It's a standard question. Say you don't know, and it will be an uphill battle to win the enthusiasm and support of the interviewer. The solution: research, research, research. The night before the interview, visit the company's Web site and pore over its financial statements, press releases and corporate mission. You can also search the company name in search engines for recent news stories regarding it.

A little too revealing

"What do you know about the company?" isn't the only question throwing job seekers off course. Unfortunately, many nervous job seekers begin rambling when confronted with a tough question, revealing potentially negative information about their skills or character. Usually it's when the most sensitive questions are asked that people don't know when to stop. These tricky questions include: "Why did you leave your last job?" "What are your strengths and weaknesses?" and "Tell me about yourself." The best thing to do is to write out your answers and do some inner preparation. If you do find yourself rambling, check yourself, repeat the question at hand, and move back to it.

It's not just what you say

The smoothest talkers could still wind up in trouble. Even if you say all the right things, your body language can send the wrong message. Tapping your pen and fiddling with papers signal to the employer that you are nervous. Slouching and leaning back indicate disinterest. Remember to smile; friendliness is crucial. Remember, if they have invited you for an interview they already believe you have the right skills, and what they are really trying to decide is if they want to work with you each day.

II. HOW TO ANSWER EMPLOYERS' QUESTIONS

The nitty-gritty of the interview is the dialogue between you and the interviewer. This part can cause you to feel a mounting sense of doom as you anticipate the questions that could cause a deafening silence during the interview. Want to avoid an interview disaster?

Below are the toughest and most common questions interviewers like to ask. Prepare a worksheet before the interview with these questions and use the suggested answers as a guide for tailoring your own responses.

Q: "What are your weaknesses?"

Don't take this literally. The secret to answering this question is being honest about a weakness, but demonstrating how you have turned it into a strength.
A: "I am very detail-oriented and in some industries that may not be a good fit. But for this accounting position, I think this trait truly will help me excel."

Q: "How would you solve this problem?"

These kinds of hypothetical questions can be risky. First of all, they may not like your answer; if they do like it, there's a chance they will steal it. That's what happened to June Sullivan when she interviewed for an activity director's position at a long-term care facility. When asked about marketing ideas, June laid out her entire plan. Well, she didn't get the job, but later recognized some of her strategies being used by the facility.

A: "I think you can increase product awareness by enacting some marketing strategies that could employ advertising, direct mail or media placements."

Q: "Describe a problem situation and how you solved it."

Sometimes it is hard to come up with a response to this request, particularly if you are coming straight from college and do not have professional experience. Interviewers want to see that you can think critically and develop solutions, regardless of what kind of issue you faced. Even if your problem was not having enough time to study, describe the steps you took to prioritize your schedule. This will demonstrate that you are responsible and can think through situations on your own.

A: "In one morning, I received two projects from two different company executives with immediate deadlines. I broke each project down, prioritized them and delegated some of the background work to other members of my team. In the end, we met both deadlines and learned new things about how we work together as a team.

Q: "Why did you leave your last job?"

Even if your last job ended badly, be careful about being negative in answering this question. An interview is not the time to dish the dirt on your previous employer. Be as diplomatic as possible. If you do point out negative aspects of your last job, find some positives to mention as well. Complaining endlessly about your last company will not say much for your attitude.

A: "The company just wasn't a good fit for my personality. But what I learned is that organizations have distinct personalities just like people do. Now I know to concentrate my job search on companies who mesh better with my work traits and offer more challenges and professional growth."

Q: "Why do you want to work here?"

Interviewers use this question to see if you have done your homework. You should never attend an interview unless you know about the company, its direction and the industry in which it plays. If you have done your research, this question gives you an opportunity to show initiative and demonstrate how your experience and qualifications match the company's needs.

A: "I want to be a part of a global company that last year alone invested $1.4 million in research and development of eco-friendly industrial processes."

Q: "Tell me about yourself."

While this query seems like a piece of cake, it is difficult to answer because it is so broad. This is a chance for you to shine—but not to tell your life history. Begin by listing your traits and accomplishments you feel are relevant for the position. The interviewer is trying to figure you out professionally so don't delve into personal information unless it relates to the position you're vying for. If you have a solid response prepared for this question, it can lead your conversation in a direction that allows you to elaborate on your qualifications.

A: "I am very creative and resourceful. I have been a sales manager for the past five years and used my creativity to devise unique incentives to keep the sales representatives motivated. Because of this my sales team earned numerous company awards."

Q: "Tell me about the worst boss you ever had."

Take the high road and don't give in to the temptation to vent any past frustrations.

A: "While none of my past bosses were awful, there are some who taught me more than others did."

Q: "What are your goals?"

This is best answered by reiterating your objective statement on your résumé. Keep to yourself your aspirations to be a vice president of marketing, own your own company or retire at forty.

A: "I want to secure a civil engineering position with a national firm that concentrates on retail development. Ideally, I would like to work for a young company, such as this one, so I can get in on the ground floor and take advantage of all the opportunities a growing firm has to offer."

Q: "Why should we hire you?"

Here's the chance to really sell yourself. You need to briefly and succinctly lay out your strengths, qualifications and what you can bring to the table. Be careful not to answer this question too generically, however. Nearly everyone says they are hardworking and motivated. Set yourself apart by telling the interviewer about qualities that are unique to you.

A: "I have five years experience in consumer marketing and understand the nuances of this industry. I can apply my online and offline marketing experience starting from day one on the job."

Q: "What accomplishment are you most proud of?"

The secret to this question is being specific and selecting an accomplishment that relates to the position. Even if your greatest accomplishment is being on a championship high school basketball team, opt for a more professionally relevant accomplishment. Think of the qualities the company is looking for and develop an example that demonstrates how you can meet the company's needs.

A: "I'd have to say probably the first time I made my sales quota. That set the standard for my work and I've achieved it now consistently for the past fourteen months."

Q: "What are your salary expectations?"

This is one of the hardest questions, particularly for those with little experience. The first thing to do before going to your interview is to research the salary range in your field to get an idea of what you should be making. Steer clear of discussing salary specifics before receiving a job offer. Let the interviewer know that you will be open to discussing fair compensation when the time comes. If pressed for a more specific answer, always give a range, rather than a specific number.

A: "In doing my research based on what the job qualifications are and my experience, I've learned that employers offer a range between $70,000 and $87,500 annually. If I did receive an offer, I would be interested in discussing this further."

POP QUIZ: Which of the following is NOT an illegal interview question?

A) You have a very unusual last name. What is its origin?
B) Have you ever been fired from a position?
C) Are you planning to start a family in the near future?
D) I notice you're wearing a Star of David necklace. Are you very religious?

ANSWER: B. While an employer can't base a hiring decision on gender, religion or national origin, your employment history is fair game.

Brainteaser questions

Remember when you took the SAT and were asked which direction a tree would fall if it were tied to the ground and then cut at the base? You probably just picked a random answer and thought, "When will I ever need to know that?"

At your next job interview, maybe.

In recent years, Google and Microsoft have famously made off-the-wall brainteaser questions part of their interview processes. What started as an innovative way to test the creativity and problem-solving abilities of applicants for technology jobs has become popular in other industries. Any position that deals with customers, whether in service or sales, might include a brainteaser or two in the interview.

Recruiters ask questions ranging from how many ATMs are in the United States to how many gallons of paint are required to paint the exterior of a three-story brownstone. Unless you happen to know the actual answer, you're probably wondering what to say.

A precise answer is rarely the goal. Just talk it out. In many cases, the interviewer doesn't even know the answer. They are interested to see the logic and problem-solving ability of the candidate. Other questions are used simply to evoke a reaction from a candidate.

Naturally, many job seekers want to know if they can give a wrong answer to these questions.

Yes, you can, and it's a simple "I don't know." A candidate who answers in this manner has indicated either an inability or unwillingness to think about a complex problem and think through the required elements of an answer.

If you know the answer and give it without talking through your thought process, you haven't shown the interviewer your problem-solving skills—which was the whole point of the question. You need to go through the logical thinking process.

Of course, not all companies include these questions in their interviews, often because they don't want to put interviewees in an awkward position or make them feel demeaned. Companies want to attract candidates, not alienate them.

Overall, the questions are more about logic than creativity. Try not to stress over these questions. A responsible employer or recruiter will not place more emphasis on a test than on the rest of the interview process and treat it as a supplement, not a deal-breaker.

A good test can tell you whether the position is a good match for you. If the answers don't come easily to you, don't overthink them in an effort to lie your way into the position. Take them as a signal that you might not be suited for the job or that you might not even want it. Keep looking for one that better suits you.

III. QUESTIONS TO ASK THE EMPLOYER

After listening to the interviewer's monologue about the company and role, you're asked a barrage of questions about your background and "future plans" praying all the while that you're delivering the "right" answers. By the time the employer asks if you have any questions, it's easy to be so drained and nervous you can only stammer out, "Nope." Not asking questions, however, is passing up a chance to stand out from the competition.

An interview is meant to be a two-way street. While the hiring manager is interviewing you to determine whether you're the best fit for the job, you should be asking questions to determine whether you would be happy in the position or with the company as well as show your interest in the position.

Think of this as a competition against the other candidates. This is your chance to shine. Employers say they are interested in candidates who ask quality questions and make intelligent conversation based on what they know about the organization. Before the interview, prepare a list of questions that demonstrate your knowledge of the company and interest in the position. Here are some good topics to cover:

The company

- What do you see ahead for your company in the next five years?

- How do you see the future for this industry?

- What do you consider to be your firm's most important assets?

- What can you tell me about your new products or plans for growth?

- How do you rate your competition?

The position's history

Asking about why the position is vacant can provide insight into the company and the potential for advancement.

- What happened to the last person who held this job?

- What were the major strengths and weaknesses of the last person who held this job?

- What types of skills do you NOT already have onboard that you're looking to fill with a new hire?

The department

Asking about your department's workers and role in the company can help you understand more about the company's culture and hierarchy.

- What is the overall structure of the company and how does your department fit the structure?

- What are the career paths in this department?

- What have been the department's successes in the last couple of years?

- How do you view your group/division/department?

The job's responsibilities

To avoid any confusion later on, it pays to gain a solid understanding of the position.

- What would you consider to be the most important aspects of this job?

- What are the skills and attributes you value most for someone being hired for this position?

- Where have successful employees previously in this position progressed to within the company?

- Could you describe a typical day or week in this position? The typical client or customer I would be dealing with?

The expectations

You'll want to know how and when you will be evaluated.

- What are the most immediate challenges of the position that need to be addressed in the first three months?

- What are the performance expectations of this position over the first twelve months?

- How will I be evaluated at XYZ company, and how often?

The next steps

At the end of the interview, don't forget to ask:

- What are the next steps in the interview process?

Pre-interview checklist

Yes, you want to wow them with your sharp new suit and your minty-fresh breath, but there are some things you need to do before the interview. Start preparing a few days before so you're not scrambling on the big day.

Make sure you:

- Bring hard copies of your résumé to give to anyone you meet at the interview.

- Leave early. You might get lost, hit traffic or need to get gas. It's OK to be early; you just don't want to be late.

- Research the company's specialty, size, market and competitors.

- Research salary so you have a realistic pay range and expectation.

- Prepare to answer all questions that we've conveniently just provided!

IV. INTERVIEW BODY LANGUAGE

Your heart feels ready to leap out of your chest. Beads of sweat build on your forehead. Your mind is racing. It's not a full-blown interrogation—although it may feel like it—it's just a job interview. While it's no secret that job interviews can be nerve-racking, a lot of job candidates spend a significant amount of time worrying about what they will say during their interview, only to blow it all with their body language.

The old adage, "It's not what you say, it's how you say it," still holds meaning, even if you're not talking. You need to effectively communicate your professionalism both verbally and nonverbally. Because watching your nonverbal cues, delivering concise answers and expressing your enthusiasm all at once can be difficult when you're nervous, here's a guide to walk you through it:

Have them at hello

Before you walk into the interview, it's assumed that you will have done the following: prepared yourself by reading up on the company and recent company news; practiced what you'll say to some of the more common interview questions and followed the "what to wear on your interview" advice. So you're ready, right?

Some hiring managers claim they can spot a possible candidate for a job within 30 seconds or less, and while a lot of that has to do with the way you look, it's also in your body language. Don't walk in pulling up your pantyhose or readjusting your tie; pull yourself together before you stand up to greet the hiring manager or enter their office. Avoid a "dead fish" handshake and confidently—but not too firmly—grasp your interviewer's hand and make eye contact while saying hello.

Shake your hand, not your body

If you are rocking back in your chair, shaking your foot, drumming your fingers or scratching your . . . anything, you're going to look like the type of future employee who wouldn't be able to stay focused, if even for a few minutes. It's a not a game of charades, it's a job interview. Here's what to do (and not do):

Don't:

- Rub the back of your head or neck. Even if you really do just have a cramp in your neck, these gestures make you look disinterested.

- Rub or touch your nose. This suggests that you're not being completely honest, and it's gross.

- Sit with your armed folded across your chest. You'll appear unfriendly and disengaged.

- Cross your legs and idly shake one over the other. It's distracting and shows how uncomfortable you are.

- Lean your body toward the door. You'll appear ready to make a mad dash for the door.

- Slouch back in your seat. This will make you appear disinterested and unprepared.

- Stare back blankly. This is a look people naturally adopt when they are trying to distance themselves.

Do:

- Sit up straight, and lean slightly forward in your chair. In addition to projecting interest and engagement in the interaction, aligning your body's position to that of the interviewer's shows admiration and agreement.

- Show your enthusiasm by keeping an interested expression. Nod and make positive gestures in moderation to avoid looking like a bobblehead.

- Establish a comfortable amount of personal space between you and the interviewer. Invading personal space (anything less than 20 inches) could make the interviewer feel uncomfortable and take the focus away from your conversation.

- Limit your application of colognes and perfumes. Invading aromas can arouse allergies. Being the candidate that gave the interviewer a headache isn't going to do anything in your favor.

- If you have two people interviewing you, make sure you briefly address both people with your gaze (without looking like a tennis spectator) and return your attention to the person who has asked you a question.

- Interruptions can happen. If they do, refrain from staring at your interviewer while they address their immediate business and motion your willingness to leave if they need privacy.

- Stand up and smile if you are on a phone interview. Standing increases your level of alertness and allows you to become more engaged in the conversation.

Say good-bye gracefully

We don't mean you have to do pirouettes out of the interview. After a few well-thought-out questions and answers with your interviewer, it's almost over, but don't lose your cool just yet. Make sure your good-bye handshake is just as confident now as it was going in. Keep that confidence going while you walk through the office building, into the elevator and onto the street. Once safely in your car, a cab or some other measurable safe distance from the scene of your interview, it's safe to let go. You may have aced it, but the last thing you want is some elaborate end-zone dance type of routine killing all your hard work at the last moment.

V. HIRING MANAGER SECRETS

If you worry about every possible way you can blow a job interview—from mispronouncing the boss's name to babbling incessantly when you don't know what else to say—you're going to walk in there feeling like you're destined to fail. True, job interviews are rife with opportunities for you to embarrass yourself, but hiring managers are more forgiving than you might think.

We consulted some hiring experts about what is really going on inside their heads when interviewing job applicants. They offered the following insights:

They like you. They really like you.

Most hiring managers come to the interview wanting to hire you. They are hoping you are the best person for the job and can start when they need you. After all, you made it to the interview didn't you?

They don't want to hear what you think they want to hear

Interviewers have gotten very smart to picking up if someone's spewing something they've memorized from a book. By only saying what they think the employer wants to hear, job candidates are simply putting on an act, and employers can see right through that. You have to be yourself in an interview and you have to be sincere.

They don't expect you to have all the answers

Employers are more interested in how you find answers to things you don't know than if you pretend to know something you don't. In some cases, the interviewer may ask a question that he or she doesn't expect you to be able to answer simply to see how you handle it. If you ever find that you don't know the answer to an interviewer's question, the best thing to do is to admit that you don't know, but either add that you could give an educated guess or provide a way you might go about finding the answer. Most important, if you don't know, don't try to fake it. Not knowing is OK. Making something up or pretending to know is not.

They want you to want them

You need to express genuine interest in the job or the company. As much as the recruiter wants to sell the candidate on the position and company, the recruiter also wants to know that the candidate actually wants to work in that position or for that company.

VI. INTERVIEW MISTAKES

You've learned the things that will blow an interviewer away, but there are still some mistakes that will sink your chances in an instant. CareerBuilder.com asked hiring managers to identify the top mistakes job candidates make. Read on about the worst qualities you can display in an interview and some real-life examples.

Lousy communication skills

A candidate who has bad grammar, talks too much or does not listen is a red flag. Being too open during the interview is a killer, too. You should be candid, but don't spill your guts with all your personal problems. And think before you speak—one candidate at a drug treatment facility asked if they drug-tested and if there was advance notice.

Poor performance or preparation

Yes, there are job seekers who don't prepare or even know what job they're interviewing for. Physical ticks like lack of eye contact or extreme gestures and movement turned off employers. Other candidates simply flaked out—answering a cell phone, eating a sandwich or jumping up out of the chair and falling down.

Negative attitude displayed

Hiring managers are turned off by unenthusiastic, bored or arrogant behavior. Using profanity, acting cocky or putting down a previous boss will quickly turn off an interviewer. One thirty-seven-year-old candidate said the only reason he was seeking a job was because his mother wanted him to.

Inappropriate appearance

Improper dress and grooming can jeopardize an interview, too. Ladies, this is not a pick-up opportunity, don't dress like you're going clubbing. Guys, jeans and a T-shirt are not acceptable. Countless hiring managers cited instances of candidates who obviously did not bathe. Think that's bad? Said one employer, "One candidate did not wear shoes to the interview. How you can forget your shoes?" Oh, and please be sober.

Lying on résumé or during interview

Do you have to be told that dishonesty is a no-no? "One guy mentioned his arrest after indicating on an application that he had never been arrested," said one hiring manager. And just in case you weren't sure, stealing from a prospective employer is also frowned upon in an interview.

BY THE NUMBERS

What are the most detrimental mistakes candidates make when interviewing?

Dressing inappropriately—51 percent
Talking negatively about current or previous employers—49 percent
Appearing disinterested—47 percent
Appearing arrogant—44 percent
Not providing specific examples—31 percent
Not asking good questions—29 percent
Providing too much personal information—16 percent

VII. DAMAGE CONTROL

Although you prepare yourself for every interview question you might be asked, there's always a possibility you'll tank. It's only natural that you overanalyze your performance, worrying that you rambled on too long about one topic or didn't say enough about another. You probably didn't ruin your chances with those little mistakes. You might just have this gut feeling that you weren't "on" and didn't present your best self. Or, if the interviewer responded to each of your answers with a furrowed brow or furious scribbling, you might have reason to worry.

Instead of dwelling on the situation and giving up hope for a second interview, get proactive and do some damage control. After all, even *American Idol*'s Simon Cowell, who's considered one of today's toughest interviewers, has been known to give a second chance more than once.

What did you do wrong?

First, you need to know what went wrong. You might have walked away knowing the interview didn't go as well as you had hoped, but you can't fix the problem until you know what it was. So think about your answers, your body language and anything else that an interviewer would notice. Refer to the first part of this chapter. Did you commit any or all of the mistakes we warned you about?

Usually one mistake won't determine whether you get the job. If interviewers notice a series of mistakes that hint at your personality and work ethic, you might be in trouble. For example, if the conversation about your work history consisted of you explaining why you left every job on your résumé, the interviewer probably wondered if you can commit to the position for a long period.

The easiest way to land your résumé in the "No" pile is to bad-mouth a former boss. You've just told the interviewer that you won't keep your negative opinions to yourself if you ever leave the company.

Also, knowing nothing about the position or company you're interviewing with demonstrates a lack of preparation and overall interest the company.

If you did any of these things or something else you know was just as damaging, decide how you can convince the interviewer you have something to offer the company. You'll have the opportunity for this in your follow-up thank-you letter.

VIII. THANK-YOU NOTES

Your interview went well: You looked professional, spoke with confidence and asked all the right questions.

Don't pat yourself on the back just yet, though. Your work's not done until you send a thank-you note to the interviewer.

Despite what many job seekers think, thank-you notes are not useless formalities. Fifteen percent of hiring managers say they would not hire someone who failed to send a thank-you letter after the interview, according to CareerBuilder research. Thirty-two percent say they would still consider the candidate, but would think less of him or her.

At this stage in the interview process, you don't want to give your interviewer a reason to choose someone else, so send the note.

Follow up with the interviewer

All job candidates should write a thank-you letter after an interview, but if things didn't go well, use it to make your case for a second chance. Employers have told us it can work.

The thank-you letter should leave a bigger impression than your initial meeting. You don't always need to send a book of poetry to get that second interview, but you do need to be just as articulate and thoughtful about what you say in your letter. This letter is your one chance to say what you wish you'd said in the interview.

Think about how the interviewer perceived you and try to erase that idea from his or her mind. Recruiters think many candidates don't view themselves as potential representatives of the company they're interviewing with. But that's exactly what you are. The way you present yourself in an interview is seen as the way you will represent the company.

In your follow-up, tell the interviewer that you know the conversation was not what either of you had in mind. Make it clear that you normally perform better and were just having an off day. You don't want to whine or beg because that is guaranteed not to get you a second chance. Just be honest about what went wrong and why you're worth a second chance.

How and when to send a thank-you note

The question becomes whether you should send an e-mail or a written letter. Job seekers and employers are still grappling with the issue. Twenty-five percent of hiring managers told CareerBuilder.com they prefer to receive only an e-mailed thank-you note. Nineteen percent want an e-mail followed by a hard copy; 21 percent prefer only a typed hard copy; and 23 percent want only a handwritten note. In the end, use your best judgment. You met with the hiring manager and got a feel for the company's environment—do what feels right.

While the business world has not reached a consensus on a thank-you note's delivery method, everyone agrees that speed counts when it comes to sending it. Twenty-six percent of hiring managers expect to receive the letter within two days of the interview, while 36 percent expect it within three to five days. Decide if you want to use e-mail, snail mail or both—then get writing.

Here are some tips to make the most of your thank-you letter:

- Keep it short.

- First, thank the interviewer for the opportunity. Second, remind the hiring manager of your qualifications. Finally, reiterate your interest in the position.

- Fill in the blanks.

- Thank-you notes are a great way to give key information you forgot to mention in the interview, so clarify any points or try to ease any reservations the interviewer might have expressed.

- Proofread carefully.

- Again, don't rely solely on your spell-checker. Double-check to be sure your note is free from typos and grammatical errors.

- Be specific.

- Don't send out a generic correspondence. Instead, tailor your note to the specific job and the relationship you have established with the hiring manager.

Keep looking

Once you've sent your letter or made the phone call, the interviewer will contact you if he or she wants a second meeting. You don't want to hound the interviewer for an answer. Instead, keep job hunting. An even better opportunity might be waiting for you.

Throughout the process, remember that you have nothing to lose by asking for a second chance. Employers, who are only human themselves, are usually willing to listen to reasons someone made a mistake and give them a second chance.

The only way you're certain not to get a second chance is if you don't ask for one. So don't sit there and torture yourself over the interview: Do something about it.

POP QUIZ: What percentage of hiring managers would think less of or outright reject a candidate who didn't send a thank-you letter after the interview?

A) 12 percent
B) 28 percent
C) 36 percent
D) 47 percent

ANSWER: D. Politeness counts: Nearly 15 percent would automatically dismiss a candidate who didn't send a thank-you note, and an additional 32 percent would think less highly of the candidate.

THANK-YOU NOTES: THERE'S A RIGHT WAY . . .

Ashley Johnson
555 North Avenue
Chicago, IL 60601

May 6, 2008

Kiersten A. Smythe
Managing Editor
A-to-Z Publications
100 Michigan Avenue
Chicago, IL 60601

Dear Ms. Smythe:

Thank you for meeting with me yesterday to discuss the assistant managing editor position at A-to-Z Publications. After discussing your plans to launch several new magazines this year, I was happy to contribute some of my creative ideas to what I'm sure will be many more successful publications for A-to-Z.

Your business plan to launch a new fashion magazine is particularly interesting to me. As you saw in my portfolio, I created a prototype for a magazine of this nature when I was an intern for *Fabulous Fashion* magazine. In conjunction with designing the layout of the prototype, I generated twenty-five story ideas, wrote three original articles, and chose the graphic details for the magazine. Because of my experience creating a magazine from scratch, I know I can make significant contributions to your new magazine's success.

Again, thank you for taking the time to meet with me. If I can provide you with any other information to help with your hiring decision, please don't hesitate to call me. You'll find my contact information enclosed. I look forward to hearing from you soon.

> Sincerely,
> Ashley Johnson
> Ashley.Johnson@abcmail.com
> (312) 555–9876

. . . AND A WRONG WAY . . .

> Ashley Johnson
> 555 North Avenue
> Chicago, IL 60601

May 6, 2008

Managing Editor
A-to-Z Publications
100 Michigan Avenue
Chicago, IL 60601

To whom it may concern:

I had such a great time meeting with you last week for my interview. I'm sorry I wasn't able to write you earlier; I've been going through a lot of personal drama and haven't really had time for this letter until now.

I just wanted to write and say THANK YOU SO MUCH for giving me the opportunity to interview at A-to-Z Publications. I swear I've sent out a hundred thousand résumés and you are just about the only interview I've had!

I am so excited for the opportunity to work with magazines!! Before our interview, I didn't even know which magazines were published by your company, but after our talk, I'm so happy to learn that I actually read a lot of your stuff. When I read my favorite magazine of yours, *GossipWeekly*, I'm always thinking to myself about all the stuff that I would change if I could. When I get this job, I will give you all of my opinions and make some major necessary changes!

I think I would be awesome for this position for many reasons. First of all, even though I don't have any writing experience, I read at least three magazines per week, so I am very "in the know" about the industry. Second of all, you probably remember from my interview that I am young and I dress really good. Since you are making a new fashion mag, I could use my fashion sense to make sure the magazine included all the latest trends because I could ask my friends about all the hot fashions they like.

Obviously, you can see that I really need this job. I hope you'll make the right decision and hire me. Please let me know as soon as you've made your decision. I hope it's the right one!

> Love,
> Ash

P.S.—I couldn't remember your name, so I hope this gets to the right person!

. . . AND A *REALLY* WRONG WAY.

(Nothing at all.)

Chapter 5

THE JOB OFFER

After weeks or months of pounding the pavement, banging on your keyboard and your head *against* your keyboard, sending out countless résumés, and meeting with employer after employer, you've received an offer. An offer for a great job. An offer you want to accept immediately.

I. WEIGHING THE JOB OFFER

Be sure to evaluate all the different factors before making the commitment to a new job. You've done the test drive and kicked the tires but you still need to read the fine print. It's not just about money (though we know that's huge)—you need to consider the whole package. As some of us learn too late, sometimes your dream job is not all it's cracked up to be.

Stop to consider these important things before you say (or scream) yes to the job offer.

1. Salary

Money isn't everything in a job; but it matters. Will you be able to pay your bills? Are you getting paid what you're worth? Have you factored in your city's cost of living? Remember, $80,000 in Chicago won't go as far as $50,000 in Danville, Kentucky.

Arm yourself by doing salary research (we'll tell you how to do that in the next section) to learn the national average salary for your position, as well as the average for your city. If the initial salary offer is less than acceptable, don't be afraid to negotiate for something a little higher.

2. Perks and benefits

Ask questions about the perks and benefits your new job could offer. If your base salary is low, are bonuses awarded to compensate for that? If so, are they based on your performance or the company as a whole? What kind of insurance will you have? Find out details about paid time off, retirement funds, stock options, etc. Inquire about any added perks, like wellness reimbursement or transportation compensation.

3. Your role

Make sure you're clear on what exactly your role will be in this new position. Do you know why they're hiring for this job? What happened to the employee before you? Do the daily activities of the job appeal to you? Will you have the opportunity to advance in the company and/or grow within your role? Don't say yes to an offer unless you're clear on what you'll be doing everyday.

4. Company culture

When you have to spend an average of 40 hours per week somewhere, you better hope it's somewhere you feel comfortable. Spending that much time in a place where you're pretending to be someone you're not, or adhering to rules and values you don't believe in is bound to catch up to you someday. Before you say yes, find out about the work environment. Are the company's values in line with your own? What's the management style? Will you have to lie or throw your co-workers under the bus to make your way to the top? If you don't feel like you'll be able to enjoy where you are, you might think about waiting for another offer.

5. Commute

If taking this new job increases your commute time, make sure you account for the time you add to your workday, the cost to fill your gas tank and the stress it adds to your life. If you spend more than three hours per day getting to and from work, you qualify as an "Extreme Commuter." A U.S. Census Bureau study, "Journey to Work," found that 3.4 million Americans endure a daily commute of at least 90 minutes each way—more than triple the national average of 25.5 minutes.

The longer drives can take their toll on the physical and mental health of workers and their families. A study by the University of California Transportation Center found that long commutes adversely affect blood pressure, mood, overall health and fitness levels, job stability and life satisfaction. Economists Bruno Frey and Alois Stutzer of the University of Zurich concur, adding that extreme commuters are on average much less happy with their lives because they lose out on social connections, hobbies and health.

POP QUIZ: According to a survey of more than 875 hiring managers, what percentage of employers say the first salary offer is final?

A) 30 percent
B) 40 percent
C) 50 percent
D) 60 percent

ANSWER: A. Thirty percent of hiring managers say they'll extend a new salary offer once if a candidate asks for it. Nearly one-in-ten say they'll extend a new offer twice or more if they really want a candidate.

II. GET PAID WHAT YOU'RE WORTH

It's a catch–22 when it comes to salary talks with a potential employer. Ask for too much and you might be dropped from consideration; ask for too little and you could be earning less than what your employer is willing to pay.

The way to escape this seesaw is to do your research and find out exactly what the position you're vying for earns in the industry you're seeking. This way, when it comes to talking cash, you have facts to back yourself up, not just the need to feed your shopping addiction.

How do you find out whether your salary is at market value for your profession, position and location? You can turn to your friends, but they may embellish their salaries, so reliability is suspect. Your parents' input as to what people make may be outdated. Finding good sources is not easy, but here are some tips for assembling information that might lead you to the answer:

Determine your needs

First, figure out what you'll need to earn each month to make ends meet. Draw up a budget for your necessities including rent, credit card bills, school loans, cell phone, car insurance and food. You'll probably also want to factor in extra money for going out with friends, clothes and savings. That's what your minimum take home pay should be ideally each month.

Do your research

With the proliferation of information on the Internet, it's now easier than ever to find salary information; the trick is knowing where to look. Here are some resources that should help you determine the salary range for any position. Remember to cross-check your findings using more than one source.

Salary Web sites

As we mentioned previously, compensation profiling Web sites such as CBSalary.com are an easy way to locate salary information in a specific region of the country. Salary Web sites generally evaluate salary information based on specifics such as expected job title, job location, experience and education of the applicant. CBSalary.com offers this service free-of-charge.

Ad hoc searches on search engines can sometimes direct you to fruitful results. A search engine query for "salary information" and "salary guides" can lead down various paths and you might get a little lost. Even better is to narrow the search by profession, say, to "accounting salaries" or "accounting salary guides."

Bureau of Labor Statistics (BLS)

The BLS collects labor-related data on specific professions as well as national trends like unemployment rates. The BLS online *Occupational Outlook Handbook* (www.bls.gov/oco/home.htm)—which contains a description of numerous jobs, along with their working conditions, the training/qualifications needed, the job's outlook and its average wages—is a great jumping-off point for investigating salaries.

Trade publications and professional associations

Association sites for a particular profession might be one of the most reliable sources of salary information. Some sites do not have salary surveys listed among their menus, but a call or e-mail to the site administrator might reveal how that information can be obtained. Trade publications often run their own salary surveys, so search their Web sites. One pitfall about trade and association Web sites: You often need to be a subscriber to access information.

Tip: If you are having problems finding trade and professional organizations to refer to, go back to the *Occupational Outlook Handbook*. At the bottom of each job details page, look under the heading "Sources of Additional Information."

Word-of-mouth

Connect with other professionals in your industry to learn more about the salary range of a position. If you don't have a personal connection to someone in the industry you're interested in, the associations and trade publications mentioned above often contain information that will help you make contact with professionals. If you're looking to advance within your own company, co-workers can be a valuable source of information. Even if a co-worker is willing to speculate about the salary range of the position you'd like to fill, keep in mind that insight is generally of the heard-it-through-the-grapevine variety, and should not be taken as fact or repeated during salary negotiations.

What comes into play

As you do your research, keep in mind that it's important to review salary data with a grain of salt. No matter what the national statistics imply, there are many factors that can result in your salary differing from the numbers you find. Remember that salary is dependent on:

- **YOUR QUALIFICATIONS:** Your work experience, skill set and educational background (including degrees and certifications) will all factor into your salary.

- **GEOGRAPHIC LOCATION:** A position in a small town will have a different salary than an identical position in a city (of course, the cost of living in each location might negate the wage disparity).

- **SIZE OF COMPANY:** Similarly, an otherwise identical job will pay differently at a small company versus a large company (however the additional responsibilities, freedoms and potential growth within a smaller company could make it a more attractive choice).

- **INDUSTRY:** Again, identical jobs in different industries will not pay the same amount. For example, an administrative assistant will typically make less at a nonprofit organization than at a financial institution.

- **ENTIRE COMPENSATION PACKAGE:** Though you may be offered a salary that is less than the amount you've researched, it's important to consider the entire compensation package that a company offers. Perhaps the salary is less, but the benefits, paid time off, tuition reimbursement or flexible hours make the position more valuable than it first appears.

BY THE NUMBERS
Forty-seven percent of workers always or usually live paycheck-to-paycheck; 21 percent who earn $100,000 or more live paycheck-to-paycheck.

III. SALARY NEGOTIATION

Salary negotiations can be tricky. Before you sign on the dotted line, be sure you understand the pitfalls and are well prepared to score the best possible salary package.

DO YOUR HOMEWORK. We can't stress enough the importance of researching salary. Understand the salary range.

BE REALISTIC. Be honest with yourself about what you can and cannot do. For example, if you are offered a job for which you don't meet all the requirements, it's unlikely you'll be able to negotiate to the top of the salary range. One major part of being realistic about what you can make is being reasonable about what skills you can bring to the table.

SCRIPT IT OUT. Plan your discussion. You should have a minimum and a maximum figure going into the negotiation. Your minimum is what you would need to get by—enough for bills, housing and food. The maximum (be realistic) should be the top of your researched pay range. Ideally, the salary you wind up with will fall somewhere in the middle.

BITE YOUR TONGUE. Don't be the first to talk about money. Wait for the hiring manager to bring it up, no matter how much you're dying to know what you could be earning in the role. When the hiring manager mentions salary, you know they are interested.

NO QUESTIONS, PLEASE. Never close with a salary question. Most interviewers will conclude their battery of questions by asking if you have any. Asking about salary shows you only care about one thing—and it's not the job at hand.

JUST THE FACTS. Postpone salary discussions until you have all the facts. If you're asked how much you expect to earn, don't give your range immediately. Ask further questions about the job requirements to gain clarity.

BE TRUTHFUL. Don't lie about your current salary. When employers do a background check, they can easily find out your previous salary. If they find you've been dishonest, that could jeopardize your offer.

MAKE 'EM SWEAT. Leverage another offer. If you have a valid offer from another employer, use it to your advantage. Tell the interviewer that you are seriously interested in the position but you do have another offer and you don't want to make a wrong decision. It's kind of a way to force an offer. Careful, this could also backfire—the interviewer might decide to cut you loose, too.

LEAVE THE DOOR OPEN. What if you really want a job, but the employer makes you a lowball offer? While cash for most is king, having a short commute and good medical benefits might matter more than a few extra dollars. Or perhaps you'd be willing to trade a couple thousand dollars for more vacation time.

FOCUS ON THE BIG PICTURE. Make sure you are taking into account whether or not the job is right for you, not just the fancy (or meager) paycheck. There are so many things to consider when taking a new job. From the company culture, to whether the job is challenging enough, to advancement opportunities, you need to weigh all of your options.

IV. WHAT TO SAY IN YOUR SALARY TALKS

If the thought of salary negotiation fills you with terror, here are some common situations and what you can say:

The hiring manager asks you immediately about salary in the interview . . .

WHAT COULD GO WRONG: Mention a salary too high, too early and the hiring manager could discount you before you have a chance to prove yourself.

WHAT TO SAY: "I'd feel comfortable learning more about the position first and discussing salary if an offer is made to me."

The hiring manager asks what your last salary was . . .

WHAT COULD GO WRONG: Unfortunately, this could cause the employer to make a lowball offer.

WHAT TO SAY: "I made $30,000 in my last position but it was also a nonprofit organization which offer lowers pay scales" or "I made $30,000 and the research I conducted indicated I have a higher earning potential with my skills."

The hiring manager asks what you want to earn . . .

WHAT COULD GO WRONG: If you don't give a range, this could either set you up for a lowball offer or cause the hiring manager to dismiss you.

WHAT TO SAY: "I investigated three salary sites and two salary surveys and the range for someone with my background and experience is between $42,000 and $47,000 a year."

The hiring manager says your salary requirements are too high for the budget . . .

WHAT COULD GO WRONG: The hiring manager could think the number is make or break for you and not extend an offer.

WHAT TO SAY: "I'm still very much interested in the position and willing to discuss this. What other benefits are available to me?"

The hiring manager says the salary requirements are too high for the position's level . . .

WHAT COULD GO WRONG: Even if the employer could pay the salary you desire, the employer could think you are cocky.

WHAT TO SAY: "Would you be willing to start me at the salary you had in mind and be open to discussing a bump in pay in six months after you've evaluated my performance?"

THE BOTTOM LINE

While we can tell you many things about job searching, there are some questions we cannot answer:

- How long will my job search take?

- Will I ever find the perfect job?

- Is there a job out there that will pay me $1 million a year to watch reruns of my favorite TV show?

What we can tell you is the truth: You need to be committed to it, tailor it to your needs and work on it continuously. It takes time and patience, but when you finally accept a new position, it will be one of the best feelings in the world.

TOUGH LOVE AT WORK—WORKPLACE FUNDAMENTALS

Whether it took you six days or six months, you've got the job. Now you need to make it work.

Gone are the days of private offices and martini lunches. These days work is all about the three Cs: cubicles, computers and collaboration. We're working in tighter quarters, communicating nonstop with everything from texting to teleconferencing and having a whole lot of togetherness with longer work hours spanning into longer happy hours.

More than ever, the way you act affects not only your reputation as an employee and a co-worker, but also your career progression. Do you know what's acceptable and what's not? Should you really be fighting with your boyfriend (who's also your co-worker) in the copy room? What would your boss say if she knew you were spending more time IM-ing your BFF than working on those weekly reports? And are you seriously wearing *that* to the office?

Perhaps you need an intro, a refresher or a major intervention. Cultivating your career and managing a positive, professional reputation depends on many things, so here's a crash course in the most important.

Chapter 6

WORK 101

There are some things every worker should know. Unfortunately, many of these things—like keeping a somewhat orderly desk or turning off your ringtone during a meeting—are long forgotten after you've gotten comfortable in your new surroundings. Here's a primer.

I. YOUR FIRST DAYS ON THE JOB

Now that the excitement of landing that coveted job has tempered a bit, you may be feeling some anxiety anticipating those first days. It's only normal. After all, you're jumping headfirst into new surroundings, meeting all new people and facing many new challenges. Follow these tips and you'll lay the groundwork for success at your new job:

SHOW UP ON TIME. Don't think because you are new you will just blend into the woodwork and no one will notice if you're a little tardy. Nothing says, "I'm a slacker," like arriving late for your first days on a new job. If you can, even show your face a little early.

DRESS APPROPRIATELY. First impressions can be lasting. Just because you're not wowing them in the interview anymore, it doesn't mean you shouldn't dress to impress. Rather than have to work twice as hard to erase the image of the rumpled or dirty shirts you wore your first week, knock 'em dead with a clean, polished look. (Not to mention that many ID photos are often taken on the first day, so this will ensure a headshot you'll be proud of.)

MEET YOUR CO-WORKERS. Make an effort to remember names. Nothing is more inviting than being greeted personally. Try to learn the names of your colleagues, including support staff, and you'll make friends fast. A good trick is to repeat that person's name when you meet him or her and associate the name with something familiar.

LISTEN. One of the best ways to learn is to listen. Consider yourself a blank slate and take note not only of information you hear in formal meetings, but also of the little nuggets shared during casual breaks or in the lunchroom.

ASK QUESTIONS. Not only does asking questions give you visibility at meetings and involve you in discussions, it's a great way to learn and demonstrate your industry knowledge.

GET INVOLVED. Even if it's just organizing a lunch meeting or a happy hour, head up a project to get your name out there and meet some of your co-workers.

COMMUNICATE. Communication is very important not only in your first few days, but every day. Just about every company has "unwritten rules," so don't be afraid to ask your co-workers for advice. And make sure you keep your boss apprised of your current projects and let her know if there is a particular project on which you'd like to work. You can't expect people to read your mind.

AVOID GOSSIP. Don't get sucked into the rumor mill. Because you're new and still relatively unknown, some colleagues may feel more comfortable venting to you. Don't respond or give unspoken credence to the barbs by laughing, nodding or displaying exaggerated facial expressions.

STAY PAST QUITTING TIME. Even though you may not have a lot of work to do yet, it couldn't hurt to stay a few minutes after the whistle blows. Don't shut down your computer at 4:59; rather stay 10 to 15 minutes after quitting time to show your commitment.

BE UPBEAT. These first days can be awkward, confusing and full of doubt. But don't let it get you down. Begin and end each day with a smile and a cheerful greeting. Your positive attitude will brighten the office.

POP QUIZ: What do hiring managers say is the biggest mistake new college grads make their first three months on the job?

A) Late to work
B) Negative attitude
C) Too much time on personal business
D) Not asking questions

ANSWER: ALL OF THE ABOVE. When asked what the biggest mistake a new grad can make on a new job, 12 percent of hiring managers said being late to work and another 12 percent said a negative attitude. Eleven percent said spending too much time on personal matters and 9 percent said not asking questions.

II. CAREER POISON

You already know how long it can take to find the right job—yet it takes just days or weeks to lose it. There are some major deal-breakers in any workplace, whether in the boardroom or on the sales floor. Beginning on day one, here are the most important career killers to avoid.

Possessing poor people skills

A little likeability can go a long way. A study by the *Harvard Business Review* found that people consistently and overwhelmingly prefer to work with likeable, less-skilled co-workers than with highly competent jerks. Researchers found that if employees are disliked, it's almost irrelevant whether they're good at what they do, because other workers will avoid them.

Not being a team player

No one feels comfortable around a prima donna. And organizations have ways of dealing with employees who subvert the team. Just ask former Philadelphia Eagles wide receiver Terrell Owens, who was suspended for the 2005 season after repeatedly clashing with and taking public shots at his teammates and management. Show you're a team player by making your boss look like a star and demonstrating that you've got the greater good of the organization at heart.

Missing deadlines

If the deadline is Wednesday, first thing Thursday won't cut it. Organizations need people they can depend on. Missing deadlines is not only unprofessional, it can play havoc with schedules and make your boss look bad. When making commitments, it's best to under-promise and over-deliver. Pull an all-nighter if you have to. It's that important.

Conducting personal business on company time

Although there are going to be times when you have to spend a little more of your workday on personal matters, the company e-mail and phone systems are meant to be used for company business. Keep personal phone calls brief and few—and never take a call that will require a box of tissues to get through. Also, never type anything in an e-mail that you don't want read by your boss; many systems save deleted messages to a master file. And we can't tell you how many poor souls have gotten fired for hitting the "Reply All" button and disseminating off-color jokes—or worse yet—rants about their boss for all to see.

Isolating yourself

Don't isolate yourself. Develop and use relationships with others in your company and profession. Those who network effectively have an inside track on resources and information and can more quickly cut through organizational politics. Research shows effective networkers tend to serve on more successful teams, get better performance reviews, receive more promotions and be more highly compensated. No-brainer, right?

Having a casual office fling

Office romances are tricky. On a good day, they end up as a long-term commitment; on a bad day, they can make tabloid editors blush. It's best to keep these private because, once out in the open, there can be consequences. If you become involved with your boss, your accomplishments and promotions will be suspect; if you date a subordinate, you leave yourself open to charges of sexual harassment. And if it ends badly, you're at risk of everyone knowing about it and witnessing the unpleasantness.

Fearing risk or failure

If you don't believe in yourself, no one else will. Have a can-do attitude and take risks. Instead of saying, "I've never done that," say, "I'll learn how." Don't be afraid to fail or make mistakes. If you do mess up, admit it and move on. Above all, find the learning opportunities in every situation. Remember, over time, risk-aversion can be more hazardous to your career than error.

Having no goals

Failure doesn't come from not reaching your goal, but in not having a goal to reach. Set objectives and plan your daily activities around achieving them. Eighty percent of your effectiveness comes from 20 percent of your activities. Manage your priorities and focus on those tasks that support your goals.

Neglecting your image

Fair or not, appearance counts. People draw all kinds of conclusions from the way you present yourself. So don't come to work poorly groomed or in inappropriate attire. Be honest, use proper grammar and avoid slang and expletives. You want to project an image of competence, character and commitment.

Being indiscreet

Cubicles, hallways, elevators, bathrooms—even commuter trains— are not your private domain. Be careful where you hold conversations and what you say to whom. Don't tell off-color jokes, reveal company secrets, gossip about co-workers or espouse your views on race, religion or the boss's personality. Because while there is such a thing as free speech, it's not so free if it costs you your job.

BY THE NUMBERS

Ever snoop at work? Get a 5-finger discount? Bend the truth just a smidge?

Most workers keep to a certain code of conduct on the job, others not so much. In a CareerBuilder.com poll, workers admitted to committing the following workplace taboos:

- Fell asleep (45 percent)
- Kissed a co-worker (39 percent)
- Stole from the office (22 percent)
- Spread a rumor about a co-worker (22 percent)
- Drank alcohol on the job (21 percent)
- Snooped after hours (18 percent)

III. TAMING WORKPLACE MESS

In today's fast-paced business world, most professionals deal with at least some office clutter. After all, finding time to straighten up is difficult when you are facing constant deadlines and preparing for a host of meetings. Despite good intentions, maintaining a well-organized workspace may not rank high on your list of priorities. But it should.

While you may not realize it, working in a messy environment can decrease your efficiency and elevate your stress level. Have misplaced sticky notes ever caused you to forget about an assignment or miss a crucial conference call? Have you ever had to frantically redo work at the last minute because you lost your original document? When your manager requests a document, has it ever taken you a lot of digging to retrieve it? If so, a workspace makeover is in order.

Decluttering your cubicle or office may sound like an arduous and time-intensive endeavor, but it's an investment that pays big dividends. Following are some simple organization tips to help you do it:

Getting organized

START WITH A CLEAN SLATE. Carefully clear off your desk, file cabinets, bookshelves and other pieces of office furniture. Use a duster and disinfectant wipes to clean areas that haven't seen the light of day in weeks, months or even longer.

DON'T FEAR THE TRASH CAN. As you review the old memos, newspaper clippings, receipts, computer disks and outdated software manuals that you've hoarded, ask yourself if you really need each item. Be honest in your assessments. If you haven't used or referred to something in more than six months—or if you forgot about it entirely—trash it. Just remember to always use a shredder when disposing of sensitive materials.

RAID THE SUPPLY CLOSET. Once you've decided what to keep, pick up folders, labels, tabs, trays, colored markers, a pencil holder and other items that will aid your organization efforts. Also consider buying a day planner or electronic organizer. It's worth the investment.

TAME THE PAPER TIGER. The more efficient you make your paper-filing system, the more efficient you'll be at managing it. People use different methods with equal effectiveness. For example, some individuals sort documents based on date, while others delineate between active and inactive files. The key is to develop a sensible, easy-to-follow system that works for you, and then stick with it.

SCRAP THE "MISCELLANEOUS" FOLDER. Be specific when naming your files. Folders labeled "miscellaneous" or "other" can easily lead to the miscategorization—and misplacement—of important documents. If you don't have a catch-all folder, you won't be tempted to use it.

DON'T FORGET YOUR COMPUTER. As you straighten out your workspace, also take time to clean up your computer desktop. A screen filled with scores of random icons creates a sense of visual chaos that can be distracting and confusing. Delete all unnecessary files and create folders as you did for your printed materials. Once you've organized this area, do the same for your e-mail inbox.

Staying organized

KEEP ONLY YOUR MOST FREQUENTLY USED SUPPLIES ON DISPLAY. For instance, have a pen and notebook nearby for jotting notes during phone calls. If you don't use an item regularly, it doesn't need to be on your desk.

GO GREEN. Save trees and decrease the number of papers to file by not printing e-mails or information from the Web unless it's absolutely necessary.

LOSE THE POST-IT PILE. Don't tape "reminder" notes to your computer monitor; they can easily get lost. Use your day planner or electronic organizer instead.

UNSUBSCRIBE. Take your name off routing slips for any publications that you don't typically read. This will help keep your inbox from overflowing.

DON'T KEEP ANYTHING ON THE FLOOR. Inevitably, objects on the ground will either get accidentally thrown out or cause you or a co-worker to trip.

SCHEDULE TIME EACH WEEK FOR BASIC WORKSPACE TIDYING. You spend hours at your desk each day. Time spent organizing will transform your workspace into one that helps—not hinders—your ability to perform your duties quickly and effectively.

And now for the touchy-feely portion of the book:

Improving Your Workspace with Feng Shui

PLANTS—Flowers and plants bring color and life into your workspace. They stimulate good energy and absorb sound. Dead or dying plants are worse than no plants at all.

WATER—The sound of water is soothing and water itself helps with the movement of chi. This can be represented by water elements, a picture of the beach, a desktop waterfall or an aquarium. Be careful of running water or fish in your workspace, though.

LIGHT—Light represents fire and symbolizes enthusiasm, passion and high energy. Fluorescent and artificial light can make you feel stagnant and depressed. If you have an overhead fluorescent, add a desktop lamp. If there's no sunlight, go outside on your break.

IV. MEETINGS

Meetings have been hailed as the No. 1 time-waster in corporate America, and—unless food is served to offset the boredom—the most tortuous part of the workday. Mind-numbing as they may be, meetings are necessary. If conducted efficiently, they're useful and can help you stand out in the workplace.

Though *you* might be making all the right meeting moves, there are always folks who struggle with the concept of "good meeting behavior." Who among us hasn't cringed as the office windbag launched into a self-aggrandizing discourse that was completely off-point? Pitied a meek co-worker who got trounced by the office bully? Or marveled at a colleague's ability to string together an array of buzzwords that mean absolutely nothing?

Whether you're the meeting leader or just a participant, prevent yourself from being "that guy" and never make these meeting mistakes:

Being unprepared

PARTICIPANT: If you receive an agenda or support material beforehand, read it. Or, contact the leader of the meeting and ask for some background info. Figure out what you'll be able to bring to the table in a discussion.

LEADER: Make sure any technical aids are working—have a back-up plan if they aren't. Confirm your meeting room; make sure it's big enough for all attendees to fit comfortably and prepare the room beforehand so you aren't wasting anyone's time. Always provide an agenda or support material in advance.

Showing up late

PARTICIPANT: Whether you're in a meeting with two people or two hundred, get there on time. Being late will damage your image and show your disrespect for others' time. Don't expect others to review what you missed if you are late.

LEADER: Don't call an "important" meeting and then make everyone wait for you to stroll in at your own convenience. Worse, don't forget about the meeting altogether and leave your co-workers waiting for you.

Being a meeting hog

PARTICIPANT: Don't talk just to talk—plan to speak when you have something useful to say. If you're asked to say something, be conscious of how much floor time you're taking to make a point. Be blunt, be brief and be done.

LEADER: It's your job to facilitate proper flow of conversation. If there's someone hogging the floor, it's up to you to keep track of the time and let others have a turn.

Sitting silently

PARTICIPANT: Refusing to participate will earn you a label you don't want: someone who lacks creativity or who can't get things done. Or, your colleagues might get the vibe that you think you're too good to offer your input. Engage in conversations, even if it's only to share one suggestion. Otherwise, don't bother showing up.

LEADER: Encourage participation. Don't hand attendees a topic and let them run with it—lead the conversation and motivate others to get involved. If no one volunteers, take it upon yourself to ask people for their questions, comments and opinions.

Expressing rude body language

PARTICIPANT: Sleeping, sighing, slouching in your chair, hair tossing/touching/smoothing, spinning in your chair, leaving the room, eating loudly and making rude gestures or facial expressions are all distracting, rude and disrespectful.

LEADER: Manage those who are being rude. Don't put anyone down, but don't tolerate disrespectful behavior.

Conducting sidebar conversations

PARTICIPANT: Having a sidebar conversation is possibly the rudest thing you can do in a meeting. Even if you're discussing the topic at hand, save sidebar conversations for after the meeting.

LEADER: If you notice attendees chitchatting, ask if there's a question or concern—this turns the attention back to the meeting's issues, and lets everyone know sidebar conversations aren't tolerated.

Arguing or putting down others

PARTICIPANT: Disagreements are fine—as long as they're appropriate. Don't make others (i.e., the boss or your co-worker) look bad. Don't contradict them, expose their mistakes in a condescending way or ignore their points altogether. If you have something to debate, do it in private and don't waste everyone's time.

LEADER: There's no need to discredit others' ideas or comments just because you are leading the meeting. Be professional when you disagree.

Leaving your cell phone on

PARTICIPANT: Cell phones shouldn't even enter the boardroom, but if they do, turn them to vibrate mode. Interrupting meeting progress with your calls is distasteful and disrespectful. If you're expecting an obligatory phone call, either skip the meeting or let everyone in the room know in advance the call might happen and excuse yourself quietly when (and if) it does.

LEADER: Same advice—leave cell phones out or turn them off.

Chewing gum

PARTICIPANT: The smack, crackle and pop of your gum are annoying, not to mention rude and unprofessional. Get rid of it.

LEADER: You want attendees to pay attention to you, not your gum-smacking.

Shutting down after the meeting

PARTICIPANT: Forgetting what you heard in the meeting is counterproductive. Hold onto support materials, and if you still have questions or concerns, contact the leader.

LEADER: Tie up all loose ends in the meeting. Reach a consensus if necessary; otherwise, summarize effectively to answer any and all questions.

NOTE TO SELF: Post these tips in meeting rooms.

V. DEFEATING DISTRACTIONS

The office: It can be a bustling hub of activity. Phones are ringing, copiers are humming and the busy buzzing of employees is everywhere. Ah . . . the sounds of a modern workplace.

While a quiet office can be an eerie signal that a company is on its last legs, too much noise can be counterproductive, unhealthy and just downright annoying. So what can you do to eliminate excess noise at work when you don't have an office door to close? Office acoustic experts say the ABCs of dealing with noise are absorb, block and cover. Here are a few ideas on applying those noise-combating techniques:

WHITE NOISE = WHAT NOISE? If colleague conversations and ringing phones have you reading the same sentence over and over, try purchasing a white noise CD to play in your computer. This means you will be listening to the lovely sound of white water rapids, the hum of a fan or just plain static to help drown out "Bobnoxious" in the cube next to you.

HEADPHONES. Bring in your headphones and plug into your mp3 player or laptop. Just try not to sing along or you'll only be adding to the office noise problem.

PLANTS. As mentioned earlier, plants are good at absorbing noise. Bring in some greenery to the office to help take the edge off the hubbub—and they look nice, too!

NONREFLECTIVE SURFACES. Make some noise of your own and consult the facilities manager about putting some noise absorption materials in your office, such as carpets, curtains, dividers or acoustic ceiling panels. It can be argued that the noise you're working in is also being transmitted directly to clients. When they call, they too will hear the pandemonium in the background.

CONFRONT THE CULPRIT. If it's just one person in the office who is making all the noise, talk to him or her and explain your situation. The person may not even be aware of being loud.

YOU ARE ENTERING A NOISE-FREE ZONE! Perhaps you and your colleagues can designate a particular conference room or area that can be used to escape the noise. It's always good to have a quiet place to consult with clients or interview candidates.

DEVISE COMPANY POLICIES. Urge your manager or HR department to enact company policies regarding cell phone ringtones, speakerphone usage, paging systems and other noise-producing activities.

NOISE-CANCELING PRODUCTS. There are many products out there that can help with the vexing problem of noise pollution. From small, lightweight headsets to varying types of earplugs, these devices can be used to reduce annoying noise.

MOVE IT AND LOSE IT. If an ill-placed copy machine is causing too much traffic, or an overburdened fax machine rings constantly, check with office services about the possibility of relocating the noise-maker. If that won't work, see if you can relocate your workstation farther away from the machines.

POSTED: BE QUIET. Simple and friendly "quiet" signs in hallways and outside conference rooms will help remind co-workers to keep it down when leaving a meeting, heading down the hallway or grabbing a cup of coffee. If none of these suggestions lowers the decibel levels to your satisfaction, then it may be time to look for a new job (perhaps at your local library).

VI. WORKING FROM HOME

Americans really like the idea of working from the comfort of home . . . a lot. If you search the phrase "work from home" on Google, 1.9

million search results appear and there are countless studies, books, chatrooms, message boards and blogs devoted to the subject. And why wouldn't anyone want a 30-second commute?

Thanks to social and economic trends, workers and employers are increasingly open to the working from home option. Technologies necessary for setting up a home office are widely available, relatively inexpensive and getting easier for people to use. And more workers are seeking flexible schedules to care for children and aging parents.

According to the "2006 American Interactive Consumer Survey" conducted by the Dieringer Research Group, the United States has 12.4 million employed teleworkers whose employers allow to work at home during business hours at least one day per month. The survey found that there are another 16.2 million self-employed teleworkers in the United States.

Nearly one-third of workers say they work from home on occasion, according to CareerBuilder data. But how much time is actually spent working when someone brings the office home?

It's not a full eight hours. Twenty-five percent of respondents who occasionally work from home admit they spend less than one hour on their office work; 53 percent spend less than three hours and only 14 percent put in a full eight hours.

BY THE NUMBERS

What are people focusing on instead of their professional duties when they are telecommuting?

- Children—22 percent
- Personal calls and surfing the Internet—17 percent
- Vegging out: watching TV and/or sleeping—15 percent
- Personal errands—11 percent
- Housework—9 percent

While working from home may improve work/life balance, it can also create a challenge to stay motivated. If you find that you fall victim to these distractions, here are some tips to make your workday more productive:

Keep to a normal schedule

Start your day as if you were going into the office. Get up at the same time, change out of your pajamas and stick to your normal morning routine. Schedule breaks and lunch just as you would if your boss were watching. Designate a certain time for personal calls, errands, housework, exercise and any other non–office-related activities. Consider setting a timer to let you know when it is time to return to your work.

Understand expectations

Make sure you understand what is expected from you when working off-site. Be sure your manager articulates the goals of your work or a specific project, what the anticipated outcomes are and the expected delivery dates. Create a list of specific goals for the day and cross them off as you complete them. This will ensure that what you wanted to accomplish actually gets done.

Think results, not hours

Although you may need to account for your hours, what your supervisor or employer is most interested in is results. The measure of a good teleworker is based on results and attainment of established objectives and goals, since these are the only factors that can often be objectively measured.

Create an efficient workspace

Don't tempt yourself by working in front of the TV or in the same room with people who may distract you. Pick a quiet room or area for your "office." Make sure you have as many of the conveniences as you would at work. Your employer will likely provide you with a good computer. If not, invest in one that has sufficient speed and memory and software compatible with that used by your employer. You'll also likely need high-speed Internet access and a reliable Internet service provider.

Be accessible

Whether you work from home or from the road, you need to be readily accessible to others when necessary. Unless you have made other arrangements, you should be just as accessible during regular business hours to clients, co-workers and management as if you were working in a traditional workplace.

Check in regularly

It's a good idea to check in with your supervisor each day you telecommute. One telecommuter found her supervisor was easily frustrated and suspicious when he called and wasn't able to reach her immediately. She learned to check in each morning via e-mail or voice mail to advise him of her schedule and priorities for the day. That way if she was meeting with clients or on a conference call, he didn't suspect that she was goofing off. You should also check voice mail frequently to retrieve any urgent missed calls.

Report your progress

Whether it is required or not, it is a good idea to submit a status report of your activity throughout the week. This will alleviate any question of your productivity and demonstrate your ability to work off-site and independently.

Schedule face-to-face meetings

If possible, schedule periodic face-to-face meetings with your supervisor to give an update on your results, progress and activities. This face time will help in reminding your manager of the "whole" person at the other end of the phone line. It will also help ensure that you are not forgotten or overlooked when new projects or promotions are under consideration.

BY THE NUMBERS: WORKING FROM HOME

Nothing beats closing a major deal or attending a company meeting in your pj's. And now, more workers have the chance to do it.

Sixty percent of employers report they currently offer flexible schedules to employees and 39 percent plan to provide more flexible work arrangements such as:

- Alternate schedules—come in early and leave early or come in later and leave later—78 percent
- Compressed workweeks—work the same hours, but in fewer days—38 percent
- Telecommuting options—33 percent
- Summer hours—21 percent
- Job sharing—18 percent
- Sabbaticals—8 percent

Chapter 7

USING, NOT ABUSING, TECHNOLOGY

Workers today are split into two eras: BT and AT. The BT (Before Technology) workers remember what it was like to work before today's hi-tech gadgets and software. They worked on typewriters or simple word processors, they used the phone and paper memos for communication and they couldn't be reached on vacation.

Then there are the AT (After Technology) workers. They are the ones who don't know the workplace without the immediate communication of e-mail, e-faxes, IM-ing. They don't know what it's like to not have the Internet at their fingertips or computers with spell-check. They worry about getting Wi-Fi on the beach to check in with work.

Regardless if you are BT or AT, you still need to be aware of the pros and cons of technology on the job.

I. E-MAIL GAFFES

The first rule of e-mail: Never say anything you don't want broadcast to the world. The second rule of e-mail: Seriously, never say anything you don't want broadcast to the world.

Examples of e-mail faux pas are endless. There was the research coordinator who bad-mouthed her boss in an e-mail . . . and sent it to the printer in her boss's office. Or the HR executive who intended to send a layoff list to her boss, but instead, sent it to "All users." How about the public relations manager who sent an off-color joke to a co-worker—but instead it went to the entire company, including national and international offices?

Here are the most common e-mail flubs to avoid at work:

Reply all

Think twice before choosing this option. Consider who really needs to hear your response. Single out the addresses of whom you need to reply. For a 1,000-person company, this practice alone could reduce 5,700 e-mails per day.

One-liners

Be careful about using e-mails to say only "thank you" or "OK." One-word e-mail replies can be easily misinterpreted. If you are replying, say more than a word or two. If you are sending a message and it applies, use "NRN" (no reply necessary).

Missing subject

Find the main point of your e-mail and state it briefly in the subject. Nobody wants to pore through several paragraphs to get to your point.

No response

Reply to every e-mail within 24 hours unless it is spam. This will not only facilitate communication and address the issue at hand, it will help you manage your inbox.

Smileys and emoticons

If you wouldn't put a smiley face or emoticon on a business letter, you shouldn't put it in an e-mail message.

Using abbreviations

Professionals should avoid using shortcuts, such as "4 u" or "Gr8," in a business-related e-mail. This is different from legitimate abbreviations like "EOD" (end of day) or "TBD" (to be determined).

Attachments

Keep attachments to a minimum. The larger the file, the longer it takes to download and the more memory it uses on the recipient's computer. Don't send an e-mail with an attachment and no body. And, don't send an e-mail referring to an attachment and then forget to attach it.

Poor editing

Proofread all e-mails for proper grammar, punctuation and spelling. Poor composition, weak writing skills, misspellings and grammar mistakes read "unprofessional." Content improvements demonstrate an average 10 to 20 percent reduction in necessary e-mail time.

Address abuse

Not everyone wants their name and information forwarded on for the world to see. Use BCC when sending a mass e-mail to varied recipients.

Adverse comments

Stay away from negative comments in e-mails. But, it can be a good way to give bad news because there's no sugarcoating—just the facts. If the news is really bad, delivering in person may be better—it shows the messenger cares about the recipient's feelings.

Remember, even when a message is deleted, it's still accessible on the hard drive. Before sending, consider what may happen if the message is read by someone else—like the boss.

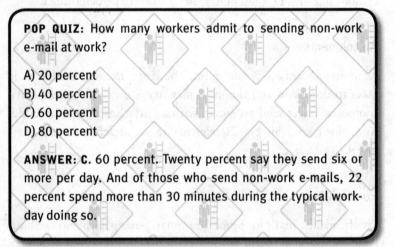

POP QUIZ: How many workers admit to sending non-work e-mail at work?

A) 20 percent
B) 40 percent
C) 60 percent
D) 80 percent

ANSWER: C. 60 percent. Twenty percent say they send six or more per day. And of those who send non-work e-mails, 22 percent spend more than 30 minutes during the typical workday doing so.

II. E-MAIL: THE GOOD, THE BAD AND THE UGLY

The good . . .

To... Joe Johnson

Cc...

Subject: Meeting Request

Good Morning Joe,

I would like to set up a meeting for the two of us to discuss hiring the new PR person sometime next week. We only need about 30 minutes and I'm free Monday, Tuesday or Wednesday afternoons mainly between 2-4 pm. What time is best for you?

We can meet in my office.

Thank you,
Janice Durkin
President
X37789

To... Core Team

Cc...

Subject: Today's Meeting

Thanks for the great meeting today. I'm really excited to get the work/life balance project started. Below is a breakdown of assignments as discussed.

Rachel
- Team lead
- Please forward weekly updates to her by Friday

Joe
- Develop business plans for each member of the team regarding individual roles.
- Running a contest for the person who comes in the highest over his or her goal for the next month

Allison
- Conduct a competitive analysis and present to group before June 15

Please let me know if I missed anything or if you need more information.
Thank you,
Michael

The bad . . .

Send	To...	Amber Jackson
	Cc...	
	Subject:	Please check the PPT you sent over this morning. Fix last graph and add conclusion.

Send	To...	Amber Jackson
	Cc...	
	Subject:	Meeting Today

RU going to be giving the update today PLZ? I'll be OOO.
BTW, George is going to be sitting in and FYI he is in a bad mood LOL.

And the ugly

	To...	Core Team
Send	Cc...	
	Subject:	Meeting Today

Thanks to all who attended the meeting today. I'm very excited that you all have decided to dedicate your lives to making this company a success. It really is the employees who drive our bottom line. I wanted to send a quick recap of the meeting via this email so if you are on a plane or travelling, you will have it at your fingertips. Thank goodness for Rachel. She has decided to take the lead and wants everyone to report into her on a weekly basis. Please send all your reports to her by the end of Friday. She said that she feels like a natural leader because she has such strong communication and management skills. I am not sure if any of you have seen her power point presentations, but she has graphs that should win awards. Maybe after this project, she can sit us all down and walk us through training. And don't forget to ask her for her apple cobbler recipe. Joe is going to develop business plans for each of you regarding your part in the project. Joe also suggested a contests for the person who comes in the highest over their goal for the next month. I agree with him. The person who comes the highest will be recognized at the company picnic this year and get a

Speaking of e-mail. . .

III. SPIES LIKE US—BIG BROTHER AT WORK

So, do you really want your boss to know that you've played more games of Facebook Scrabble than you've made sales calls? Or that you've done all your holiday shopping online while at work? Careful there—today's employers are keeping tabs on their employees in more ways than you can probably imagine. This includes checking employee phone calls, e-mail messages, Internet connections and computer files.

In its research, CareerBuilder.com found that firms do record and review employee communications and activities on the job. Half of employers say they monitor employees' online activity—23 percent monitor both time spent online and content, 19 percent just monitor content and 8 percent monitor time spent. One-third monitor employee e-mails.

Companies are increasingly creating Internet and e-mail usage policies, covering violation of company policy, inappropriate or offensive language, excessive personal use and breach of confidentiality, among other things. And they're increasingly putting those policies into action. Nearly one-in-five employers said they have fired an employee for using the Internet for non-work activities. Another seven percent said they have fired employees for sending non-work e-mail.

You can't cry foul. If an employer makes it known that they monitor, no matter how obscure, you must adhere to it. So if privacy— and keeping your job—concerns you, follow these tips for work:

Review your company's handbook

Every company has a list of policies available to its employees. When you get a new job, your human resources department should make you aware of these policies. If you don't remember them, now's a good time to brush up on what's acceptable and not on the job.

Don't use company e-mail for private messages

Although it may be tempting to forward the latest joke or urban legend to your colleagues, resist the urge. Someone in your organization—usually the network administrator—is watching all of the e-mails that come and go. Is this fair? According to experts, if your employer owns your e-mail system, the company may review its contents.

Always assume your messages will be shared with others

It's all too easy for the recipient to hit "Forward" rather than "Reply" and send your message on to others. If the contents of your e-mail messages are private, pick up the phone and call the recipient instead of using e-mail.

Keep your passwords private

If you don't want others to have access to your computer while you're out of the office, don't share your passwords. Keep them in a secure place where only you can find them.

Stay off sensitive Web sites while at work

Although you may think you are cruising the 'Net inconspicuously, every time you visit a site you leave an electronic fingerprint. Your computer screen may also be in plain view of others who walk by your workspace. Visiting credit management sites, managing your bank account online, or shopping for lingerie could have the whole office talking about what you're viewing on your monitor.

Turn off your computer

When you step away from your desk, turn off your computer. Anyone can click on your navigation bar to view the Web sites you've visited recently. Or worse, if you leave your e-mail open, a passerby could read your mail or even send a message under your account.

Pay your bills at home

If you don't want your co-workers to know how much you owe on your credit cards or the size of your mortgage, keep your bills at home. These are private documents that your co-workers and employer do not need to see, and that don't need to go through the corporate mailroom.

Keep your paycheck away from wandering eyes

Put your paycheck in your pocket or purse as soon as you get it. Given the popularity of direct deposit these days, most people don't give payday a second thought. That can be a problem when paychecks are left lying around. Consider Kathy, an account manager at a national travel company. She recently moved to another cubicle and the co-worker who now occupied her empty desk found one of her old paychecks, opened it and shared the amount with others in the office.

Report to work on time

If you think you can pull a fast one and send an e-mail that appears to have been sent first thing in the morning, remember that e-mails contain time stamps and can indicate where they were sent from. Also, thanks to security key card systems used for office building access, management can track what time you came into the building and reported for work. When needed, they can use these reports to implicate tardy employees.

Don't use a company-issued credit card for personal purchases

Many sales reps and executives receive corporate credit cards for business-incurred expenses. If you don't want the accounting department to know what size undies you wear, don't shop for clothing and other personal items with the company card.

If you are concerned about privacy and monitoring practices at your company, re-read your company handbook manual or ask your human resources department. Most businesses alert employees to the possibility that e-mail messages or online activities may be tracked. Keep in mind that your purpose at work is to—well—

work and realize that it's better to be safe than sorry. If you keep your personal e-mails to a minimum or avoid them altogether, make as few personal phone calls as possible and stay off the Internet, privacy shouldn't be an issue for you.

BY THE NUMBERS
Posting on your social networking page or blog when you should be working? You're not alone. Nearly two-in-five workers (37 percent) have a social networking profile. One-third (33 percent) of those with a profile spend time on their social networking page during the workday with 9 percent spending 30 minutes or more. Additionally, one-in-ten workers (12 percent) have a personal blog, but only 20 percent update it at work. Of those who blog at work, only 6 percent spend a half hour or more blogging.

IV. IM-ING AT WORK

Once considered taboo among business communications and used mainly by Gen-Xers to chat with friends, instant messaging, or IM-ing, is gaining wider acceptance within corporations as a quick and efficient means of communicating with co-workers and clients.

Analyst house IDC reported more than 28 million business users worldwide used enterprise instant messaging products to send nearly 1 billion messages each day in 2005. But, are all of those IMs sanctioned by their companies?

Whether or not your organization has implemented a formal IM policy, follow these suggestions when IM-ing at work and it will be NBD (no big deal), simply BAU (business as usual).

FIND OUT IF YOUR COMPANY HAS AN IM-ING POLICY. If so, make sure you understand the sanctioned uses of IMs, the content guidelines as well as specific rules for both sending and receiving IMs and attachments.

TAKE ADVANTAGE OF IM PRIVACY. In many open-office environments IMs offer employees a chance to communicate without disturbing fellow co-workers or letting them in on the conversation. Before you start typing, however, read the next entry.

UNDERSTAND THAT YOUR MESSAGES MAY BE REVIEWED. Just because they're instantaneous and you delete them quickly doesn't mean they can't be monitored by the organization or archived by the recipient. So refrain from including personal data, confidential information or any information you don't want repeated.

BE VIGILANT OF VIRUSES. Many IM products are available to download free. If you download free IM software, make sure your IT department can enact the proper security measures so the company network is not at risk for viruses or breaches.

AVOID CUTESY IM SCREEN NAMES AT WORK. Remember to always maintain a professional image. Clients don't want to be sending informative messages to 2HOT4U.

FOLLOW ACCEPTED IM PROTOCOLS. Microsoft cites 78 percent of IM-ers like the faster response they get from IM-ing versus e-mail. So keep your messages brief.

KEEP PERSONAL AND PROFESSIONAL CONTACTS SEPARATE. Maintain your "buddy lists" separate from your work contacts to ensure neither receives inappropriate information.

CAREFUL HOW YOU SAY IT. While the nature of IMs is casual and conversational, remember you are at work, so keep the messages appropriate.

KNOW WHAT YOU'RE SAYING. Before you use an IM abbreviation, make sure you really know what the letters stand for. To learn the lingo, search for "text abbreviations" or "IM abbreviations" online.

AVOID GETTING EMBROILED IN GOSSIP. The lightning fast speed of IM-ing makes for a turbocharged rumor mill. Avoid the scuttlebutt or you most surely will get burned.

SET YOUR AWAY MESSAGE. Just as you would post an out-of-office message on your e-mail, you should also include an away message. Indicate that you are in the office that day, but not available to respond to IM immediately.

> **BY THE NUMBERS**
> One-in-five workers (21 percent) report they send instant messages while at work. Of those who IM, 45 percent say IM-ing makes them more productive.

V. CUTTING THE E-LEASH

After months without a day off, it's official: You need a vacation. But you feel you just can't leave the office for a long weekend, much less five days or—gasp!—two weeks. You ask yourself: "Will the office survive without me?" "What if I'm replaceable?" or "Will people resent me if I take some time off?" Instead of chancing it, you'll just check your e-mail a few times, leave your cell phone number in case someone needs to contact you, and dial into your weekly conference call.

THE E-LEASH

About 20 percent of workers stayed in touch with the office during their vacation this year. While only 9 percent of workers say their employers expect them to check voice mail or e-mail on vacation, others may feel the pressure to do so anyway.

Work can be demanding, but taking it all with you just brings the stress to a new location. Cell phones, pagers and other electronic devices can create an e-leash of sorts. And then there's good, old-fashioned guilt: 14 percent of workers report feeling guilty about missing work while on vacation.

There are a host of reasons why employees feel compelled to forgo a vacation or obsessively check in with work. Some may fear if they are gone and things go smoothly, it will send a message that they aren't needed. Others worry that business won't be conducted properly or key projects will fall apart.

Planning ahead, managing expectations and setting boundaries with your co-workers are key to making sure you get the break you need. To enjoy a stress-free and work-free vacation, try these tips:

LEAVE A ROADMAP. A few weeks before you leave, start recording important information, key contacts and any deadlines that will come up while you are gone. If you leave co-workers with a guide that will help them address questions that arise and keep things moving forward, they will be less likely to contact you on vacation and you will be less likely to walk into a war zone when you return.

STICK TO AN ITINERARY. While it's best to leave the office at the office, if you must do work, set limits and boundaries for yourself and your co-workers. Don't let activities on vacation be interrupted by work. Instead set aside a half hour each day to think about work and stick to it. Instead of having co-workers call you, tell them when you are going to check in, so you can control the time allotted.

THINK BIG. If you have a big project and a great vacation planned for the same week, you can expect one of the two to give. Schedule the dates before and after the big stuff to lighten your load and enjoy your time off.

WHAT IF YOU'RE THE BOSS? If you're working for yourself, make sure you anticipate your busy seasons by reviewing your previous sales and current situation. Save vacation time for slower periods and make sure to notify customers in advance.

TIPS FOR NON–E-MAIL TECHNOLOGY

OUTGOING VOICE MAIL MESSAGE—Speak clearly and ask the caller to leave a purpose for the call, phone number and e-mail address.

LEAVING VOICE MAIL MESSAGES—Speak clearly, give the purpose of your call and leave your name, phone number and e-mail address.

SPEAKERPHONE—General rule of thumb: Don't use this unless you are in an enclosed room.

VIDEO CONFERENCING—Remember that even though some of the party isn't in the room, you are on camera. Body language, looks, eye-rolling and daydreaming can all be picked up.

Chapter 8

EXCUSE ME? CALLING IN SICK AND COMING IN LATE

Here's the situation. You went to the ball game last night. Your team won and you stayed out a little bit later than you should have. Fast-forward six or seven hours and that alarm is going off way too soon. What do you do?

A: Do you call in sick with a raging episodic tension headache causing pain in your right lobe, chronic fatigue and sensitivity to light? (Thank you, WebMD!)

B: Or, do you buy some time by cooking up an elaborate tale that involves checking the morning's traffic conditions, implicating your children and cursing the inventor of orange juice. (At least you didn't blow off the whole day.)

Here's what some of your cohorts are doing.

I. TAKING TARDINESS TO THE NEXT LEVEL

If you tend to suffer from a lack of punctuality, you're not alone—15 percent of workers say they arrive late to work at least once a week. One-in-five admit to making up fake excuses to explain their tardiness.

A case of the Mondays

The day workers are most often late? Not surprising, 64 percent of employers say Monday.

Most of us make up excuses in fear of repercussions. Forty-three percent of hiring managers say they don't care if their employees are late as long as their work is completed on time and with good quality—but others aren't so lenient and would consider firing an employee if it happens multiple times. The key is to know your individual manager's expectations and take the time to learn your employer's culture and policies.

Think you're being sly with the excuse you gave your boss? Guess again. While the majority of hiring managers don't typically question the validity of the reasons provided, 27 percent say most of the time they don't believe the excuses.

Here are some of the most unusual excuses employees have offered for arriving late to work, according to employers surveyed:

- "While rowing across the river to work, I got lost in the fog."
- "Someone stole all my daffodils."
- "I had to go audition for *American Idol*."
- "My ex-husband stole my car so I couldn't drive to work."
- "My route to work was shut down by a presidential motorcade."
- "I wasn't thinking and accidentally went to my old job."
- "I was indicted for securities fraud this morning."
- "The line was too long at Starbucks."
- "I was trying to get my gun back from the police."
- "I didn't have money for gas because all of the pawn shops were closed."

- "I dreamed that I was fired, so I didn't bother to get out of bed."
- "I had to take my cat to the dentist."
- "I went all the way to the office and realized I was still in my pajamas and had to go home to change."
- "I saw that you weren't in the office, so I went out looking for you."
- "I couldn't find the right tie, so I had to wait for the stores to open so I could buy one."
- "My son tried to flush our ferret down the toilet and I needed to tend to the ferret."
- "I ran over a goat."
- "I stopped for a bagel sandwich, the store was robbed and the police required everyone to stay for questioning."
- "A bee flew in my car and attacked me and I had to pull over."
- "I wet my pants and went home to change."
- "Someone was following me, and I drove all around town trying to lose them."
- "My dog dialed 911, and the police wanted to question me about what 'really' happened."
- "My girlfriend got mad and destroyed all of my undergarments."
- "I woke up and thought I was temporarily deaf."
- "I just wasn't 'feelin' it' this morning."
- "I was up all night arguing with God."
- "A raccoon stole my work shoe off my porch."
- "I super-glued my eye thinking it was contact solution."
- "I was putting lotion on my face when my finger went up my nose causing a nosebleed."
- "A prostitute climbed into my car at a stop light, and I was afraid my wife would see her and think I was messing around . . . so I got out of the car."

POP QUIZ: What is the biggest cause of workplace tardiness?

A) Long commute
B) Traffic
C) Getting the kids ready for school
D) Felt sick
E) Fell back asleep
F) Forgot something at home

ANSWER: B. When asked to identify the primary cause for coming in late, more than 32 percent of workers claimed traffic was the culprit. Falling back asleep was the reason cited by 17 percent, while 7 percent pointed to a long commute as the main cause. Other popular reasons included getting kids ready for school and daycare, forgetting something at home and feeling sick.

II. THE ART OF PLAYING HOOKY

Did you hear the one about the woman who couldn't go to work because her chickens' feet were frozen to the driveway? It's not a joke—it's an actual excuse given to a boss.

Gone are the days when an employee called in sick and coughed a little to make the story believable. Today, workers give a variety of excuses when they stay home from the office. And they're doing it a lot.

Almost one-third of employees admitted to calling in sick to work even though they weren't ill, according to CareerBuilder.com data. Fortunately for them, the majority (75 percent) of employers believe their employees are sick when they say they are.

But some bosses aren't falling for it.

Thirty-five percent of employers checked up on their supposedly sick employees. The majority (67 percent) of those suspicious bosses demanded a note from the doctor. Fifty-nine percent called the worker at home, and a determined 14 percent actually drove by the employee's home.

To lie or not to lie?

So what should you tell your boss if you need a rest but there's not a holiday in sight?

Honesty is the best policy. If you're a strong employee and you're truthful about the time you need off, your employer is likely to give it to you. But if you get caught in a lie, you risk your reputation and possibly even your job.

Luckily, many employers are beginning to understand that an employee doesn't have to be suffering from the flu to need a day off. Employers are placing a greater emphasis on work/life balance, offering more opportunities for employees to recharge and return to the office more productive.

Mental health days, which allow employees to stay home from work to escape the stress and chaos of the office, are gaining acceptance in the workplace. Sixty-nine percent of surveyed employers consider mental health days acceptable uses of sick leave.

The next time you call in sick—whether you have the flu or a desire to stay in your pajamas until noon—you can decide if you want to tell the truth or a little white lie.

If you choose to lie, here are the most unusual sick day excuses bosses have revealed to CareerBuilder.com:

- "While at my sister's wedding, I chipped my tooth on a mint julep, bent over to spit it out, hit my head on a keg and was knocked unconscious."
- "While at a circus, a tiger urinated on my ear, causing an ear infection."
- "My dog isn't feeling well, so I tasted his dog food and then got sick."
- "Someone put LSD in my salad."
- "My roommate locked all my clothes in a shed for spite."
- "I'm too upset to come to work because my favorite *American Idol* contestant was voted off."
- "I'm not feeling well and want to rest up for the company's holiday party tonight."
- "I was poisoned by my mother-in-law."
- "I'm feeling all the symptoms of my pregnant wife."
- "I broke my leg snowboarding off my roof while drunk."
- "My wife said I can't come into work because I have a lot of chores to do around the house."
- "I'm too drunk to drive to work."
- "I had to help deliver a baby on my way to work." (Employee was not in the medical profession.)
- "God didn't wake me." (Employee didn't believe in alarm clocks and thought a higher power would wake her when she was ready.)
- "The ghosts in my house kept me up all night."
- "I forgot I was getting married today."
- "My bus broke down and was held up by robbers."
- "I forgot to come back to work after lunch."
- "My brain went to sleep and I couldn't wake it up."
- "My monkey died."

III. NO EXCUSES: WHEN YOU SHOULD TAKE A SICK DAY

Despite the incidents of faking it, people don't have a problem coming to work when it's the real thing.

Eighty-seven percent of employers report that sick employees who show up to work are suffering from short-term illnesses such as a cold or flu, which can be easily spread, according to findings of the 2007 CCH Unscheduled Absence Survey.

Not all there

Employers are beginning to realize this trend, known as "presenteeism," is producing a significant drain on productivity. This lost productivity occurs when employees come to work suffering from any kind of illness or other medical condition, and are not fully functioning.

The failure to take time off to regain your health can actually lead to longer absences because health worsens; and as an illness spreads within the workplace, additional workers can be affected, raising the total employee absence time.

Health problems that result in presenteeism are relatively harmless, including seasonal allergies, asthma, headaches, depression, back pain, arthritis and gastrointestinal disorders. But when people don't feel 100 percent, they simply don't perform at their best and are less able to work effectively with others.

Unfortunately, it's harder to identify. You know when someone doesn't show up for work, but you often can't tell when, or how much, poor health hurts on-the-job performance.

Spreading the love

Another pitfall? Contagious workers can infect other workers. Furthermore, workers from one company can infect workers in another company. For example, the contagious delivery driver who visits an office could not only drop off an important package, but can also deliver a slew of germs from the workplaces visited that day.

If so many people take such great pains to call in sick, why are they going to work when they actually are sick? Sixty-five percent of respondents said it's because they have too much work/deadlines. Fifty-six percent say there is no one available to cover workload; 55 percent don't want to use vacation time; 49 percent want to save sick time for later in the year; and 49 percent report fear of discipline.

So don't be a hero. Stay home. If you feel like you can't fully detach yourself from work, be available by e-mail and voice mail.

Chapter 9

WORK DON'TS

When you're with your buddies at a ball game, it might be completely acceptable to belch and swear loudly. Or when you're home and use the last paper towel on the roll, it's your prerogative to replace it immediately or not. If you want to share the latest gossip with your friends about the girl you all hated in high school, go right ahead.

Whether or not this is proper social conduct is a matter of opinion, but we're talking about work here. And one thing's for certain, while these behaviors might be normal among your friends or tolerated at home, they are not acceptable on the job.

In this chapter, we'll talk about workplace behavior, your overall professionalism and how you carry out your day-to-day duties.

I. IT'S NOT THEM, IT'S YOU

When you walk into the breakroom, do the lively conversations stop? Do the groups quickly disband as everyone scrambles to head back to their offices? Do you think to yourself, "Was everybody's break really over or were they just trying to avoid me?"

Some people are truly hazardous to others' mental, emotional and physical health—what some call toxic personalities. If you are getting the cold shoulder from your co-workers, it could be because of your toxic behavior. If any of the following situations describe you, they might be the reason you feel left out:

"The sky isn't really blue—it's actually *cyan*."

Does this sound like something you would say? Do you incessantly spout unnecessary or obscure information that would make a *Jeopardy!* champion jealous? Are you constantly correcting people? Lose the "know-it-all" attitude or you'll make a career of lunching alone.

Break time

If your co-workers want to find you, they never bother checking your desk. You're never around because you're always chatting up your colleagues or taking a break in the lobby, the kitchen or any one of your buddies' cubes. Don't forget, there's a reason it's called work.

Workaholic wannabe

Do you mosey in late, take extra long lunches and don't really start to roll up your sleeves and dig into some serious work until about 2 p.m.? Then, do you make sure everyone sees you working past 5 p.m.? Well you're not impressing anyone; rather you're annoying those who already have put in a full day before you even get warmed up.

"I'm not one to gossip but . . ."

You're very good at filing away information—about everyone in the office! If you want to keep friends, learn to keep a secret. If people know you talk about others, they won't trust that you'll leave them alone.

Devil's advocate

Do you feel compelled to take the other side of every argument just to make a point? Well, stop it! Nothing is more exhausting for your co-workers than knowing you're always ready to challenge them, no matter what they say.

Mr. Un-clean

Leaving dishes in the sink, old food in the fridge, food splattered inside the microwave and crumbs on the break table is a surefire way to annoy fellow workers. Clean up your act.

What's that on your nose?

Do you constantly follow your boss around, laugh at all her jokes and drop her name in countless conversations? If so, then you are a brownnoser. Working in an office does require a certain amount of "schmoozing" the boss, but you don't have to tie yourself up in a pretzel to impress her—while alienating everyone else in the office.

Big mouth

You are never at a loss for words, and engage in never-ending idle chatter about yourself, your parents, your kids, your kids' friends, their parents, even strangers. You babble on with endless insignificant details about anything and everything. Practice biting your tongue and let others do the talking for once before people start avoiding you.

Laying it on too thick

Whether you are embellishing a story to impress your peers or conjuring up a phony excuse for a late assignment, your co-workers can never really trust what you say. Quit your exaggerating because when you do have something truthful to convey, most are skeptical.

Everything's a competition

You see every occasion as an opportunity to outwit or surpass your co-workers. If someone tells you how hard they worked today, you'll lament about how much harder you worked. Whenever someone shares good news, you can always one-up them. Sure you want to look good, but there's a difference between sharing information and showing off.

> **TMI! WHAT NOT TO SHARE OR DISCUSS WITH YOUR CO-WORKERS: SALARY INFORMATION**
> What you earn is between you and human resources. Disclosure indicates you aren't capable of keeping a confidence.

II. TURNING YOUR IRRITATING BEHAVIOR AROUND

Let's face it, not everyone gets along perfectly. To be successful in your work, you at least need the respect and support of others—your customers, suppliers, co-workers and management. But sometimes, despite your best efforts to win their support, bad habits creep into your daily work life and drive others crazy.

While you may not care what Bob down in accounting or Mary the HR director thinks of you, it's important to remember that

Mary may go on to become the potential new boss you have an interview with. And one day Bob just may be in charge of auditing your expense receipts at your future employer.

Here are ten surefire ways to make sure your efforts to win their support don't backfire. If any sound familiar, you could be leaving your co-workers fuming.

Thinking it's always all about you

Are you preoccupied with your own career path and looking good at the expense of others? Do you put others down while you pump yourself up? Instead, conduct yourself in such a way that other people will want to see you succeed—let their genuine support and admiration of who you are pull you to success.

Answering cell phone calls during meetings

A surefire way to aggravate people is to consistently respond to calls, e-mails and pagers when in conversation with others. This sends a message that they are less important than the caller. Let the calls go and return them when your current conversation is over. If you are expecting an urgent call, alert those present. They will appreciate that you value their time and that you stay focused on matters at hand.

Sending voice mails that go on and on and on

At the end of a voice message, replay it and hear how you sound. Difficulty in getting to the point? Just like giving a speech, state your objective or main message first and follow it with brief, supporting sub-points. Some people prefer voice mail, some e-mail—each workplace has its own expectations.

Acting like a bureaucrat

Do you drag out turnaround times and play control games? Do you create obstacles or barriers for others to do their work? Making mountains out of molehills is another surefire way to alienate people. Teach people how to navigate your organization efficiently, knowing when to stick with the rules and when to break them.

Reading the newspaper or hammering on your laptop during training sessions or meetings

Yes, there are way too many meetings and you've got more important things to do. Yet doing irrelevant tasks when there is a set agenda sends a clear message that this event or these people are unimportant to you. Instead, be fully focused—chances are if you completely engage, you will make important contributions while you show you are a committed team player.

> ## TMI! WHAT NOT TO SHARE OR DISCUSS WITH YOUR CO-WORKERS: COST OF PURCHASES
> The spirit of keeping up with the Joneses is alive and well in the workplace, but you don't want others speculating on the lifestyle you're living—or if you're living beyond your salary bracket.

"I'm like, ya know . . ."

You are your words; even more so in virtual relationships. You may be communicating with people worldwide who know you only by the sound of your voice or the tone of your e-mails. Become conscious of how you use language and stop communicating in ways that cause you to sound inexperienced or unprofessional. Ask those you trust and respect for feedback.

Doing your bills at the office

Whether you are paying your bills, planning your wedding or placing an online order for a special gift, avoid doing them on office time. People understand short personal calls and respect emergencies, but they don't appreciate seeing you get paid to manage your life.

Skirting around the dress code

Ask ten companies to define business casual and you have ten different definitions. Dressing for work has never been more complicated—especially if you work at multiple locations. Prioritize matching your customer's dress code; and if visiting more than one on a given day and the codes conflict, go for a classic, neutral look and be prepared to flex—adding or losing a jacket or tie between locations.

Taking it too easy on telecommute days

Run a few errands and throw in a load of laundry? Hey, you're a hard worker and deserve work-life balance. Telecommuting can be a tremendous win-win, but if you stretch it to its limits, you may blow the policy for yourself and others. Meet your deadlines, be readily available during business hours, and do great work—skip the temptation to make it appear like you are working when you're really not.

Acting unethically

It's easy to draw the line on major violations but watch for the subtle ways you may be pulling others in the wrong direction to achieve goals—massaging numbers or data, violating copyright or providing misleading information. Raise the ethics bar high and hold yourself and others to it.

> **TMI! WHAT NOT TO SHARE OR DISCUSS WITH YOUR CO-WORKERS: INTIMATE DETAILS**
> Don't share intimate details about your personal life. Co-workers can and may use the information against you.

III. WORST THINGS TO SAY AT WORK

Over time, you've probably learned what not to say in a relationship. "Are you losing your hair?" "Yes, you do look fat in that dress." "I should give my old boyfriend a call." "You're just like your mother."

When it comes to the workplace, however, you might not realize there are plenty of things you can say to damage your relationships or even your own career. An off-the-cuff remark that you think went unnoticed, for example, might be the first thing your boss remembers when he thinks about you.

Remember: Just because you don't end up sleeping on the couch, it doesn't mean your mouth can't get you in trouble. For the sake of your career, here are ten things you should avoid saying at work.

"That's not my job."

If somebody comes to you with an issue, there's probably a reason. It might be your responsibility or they might just value your input. Either way, use the situation to prove you're a team player and a problem solver. Plus, it pays to earn some good office karma because you never know when you'll need help from other colleagues.

"Yeah, no problem." (If you don't mean it.)

If you take on a task with a smile but have no intention of actually completing it, you're going to earn a reputation as an unreliable person. If you know you can't or won't complete the project, be honest about it. Your colleagues are relying on you, so your decision not to follow through impacts their jobs, too.

"Don't tell anyone I said this, but . . ."

If it's really a secret, keep it to yourself. Whether you know someone's about to get fired or what the boss's salary is, you're going to get credit for spreading the news. You're not exempt from being the subject of office chatter, either. Don't expect your gossip-loving coworker to suddenly have tight lips when it comes to divulging your secrets.

"I haven't had a raise in four years."

Just because you have longevity with your employer, it doesn't necessarily warrant a raise. Asking for a raise because of how long it's been since your last one will only tell your boss that you want more money, not that you deserve it. Instead, highlight the accomplishments you've made in the last four years. Prove the raise is merited.

"It's not my fault."

When your boss comes to you with a problem, the last thing you want to do is deflect blame to someone else. Maybe it isn't your fault, but remember that you're not in a courtroom and nobody's really looking for the culprit right now. All that matters is making sure the problem is solved and doesn't happen again. You can deal with the real issue later, but you'll just make yourself look worse if you spend more time finger-pointing than problem solving.

"To be honest with you . . ."

First, any time this phrase is used, you know something negative is going to follow. More important is the message it sends to others. Why do you have to identify when you're being honest? Are you not honest at other times at work? Instead, without being rude, say what you need to say in a straightforward manner.

"Whom did you vote for?"

The old adage that you shouldn't discuss politics is as true today as ever before. While it's great that you're an active citizen performing your civic duty, save the politics for your personal blog. Even if the conversation doesn't result in an argument, you never know who you're making uncomfortable or who will hold your views against you. In a sea of cubicles, there are more people listening to your conversation than you think.

"I got so trashed last night . . ."

You're probably not the only person in the office to indulge in a drink (or a keg) now and then, but you're probably the only one bragging about it to your boss. Although your night of binge drinking didn't force you to call in sick this morning, it can create the image of an unreliable partier who forgot to leave the beer bong in the dorm room.

"I just didn't have enough time for that."

In case you didn't realize, everybody's pretty busy these days. When your boss asks you to do something, chances are it's not really an option. If your main concern is accomplishing the task on time, you explain the situation. Mention how busy your schedule is but that you can accommodate the request if some other projects are moved around. You'll show that you take each assignment seriously and only want to turn in your best work.

" . . . or else."

Giving anyone in the office an ultimatum rarely ends in success. Whether you say it to a colleague or your new intern, you'll only gain enemies and earn a reputation for being difficult. If cordial requests don't work and threats are the only way to get things done in the office, you need to re-evaluate your work environment.

IV. WHAT YOU WEAR . . . HEAD-TO-TOE TABOOS

Skin. Everyone has it. And one glance at TV, movies and magazines reveals how much people love to flash it.

But unless you're working in a very few select industries, flashing too much in the office says, "I'm inexperienced, unprofessional and hoping people will not notice I have no real skills for this job."

Once you get the reputation as a sultry dresser, it may be difficult to shake that image and ever be taken seriously by your colleagues. Consider this story one supervisor told us:

Young and ambitious, Olga showed up for her first day of work at a transportation company wearing a low-cut top, fishnet stockings and stiletto heels so high she could take only mincing steps. Olga was a head-turner all right—but for the wrong reasons.

After watching Olga get ogled for three days, her new boss asked Beth, a young HR manager, to speak to her about her wardrobe. "I tried to impress upon her the image of trust and credibility the firm was trying to project," Beth explained earnestly. "I told her that while her outfits were great for clubbing, they were sending the wrong signals here at work."

Olga's response shocked her. "She unabashedly told me that she couldn't help it if people felt threatened or turned on by her. She was who she was and those people bothered by it were probably older, fatter and jealous."

Yes, the workplace has become more casual but there really are limits.

While what you wear to work has its exceptions depending on your work environment, most image consultants and corporate executives agree that there are basic standards everyone should follow.

Before you walk out the door today, make sure you're not sporting:

UNDERWEAR AS OUTERWEAR. Camisoles or visible bra straps and lingerie scream "Eek!" not "Chic!"

WORKOUT GEAR. Save your muscle shirts and spandex for the gym.

SOILED, STAINED OR RUMPLED CLOTHING. Neatness counts. Better to wear less expensive clothing that is immaculately cleaned and pressed than to sport designer grunge.

SHORTS. Whether of the Bermuda or Daisy Duke variety, wearing shorts to work is just plain wrong.

TATTOOS. These days, tattoos seem almost mainstream, but many people are still put off by them. Best to keep yours under wraps or disguised with a heavy spray-on makeup made expressly to conceal tattoos.

EXTREME HAIR COLOR. Natural looking highlights are fine, but never dye your hair blue, magenta or other colors not found in nature.

TOO MUCH COLOGNE. A strong scent is a turnoff to most people. Best to forgo fragrance and opt for the clean smell of soap.

LONG, FAKE OR WILD-COLORED NAILS. Keep your nails short and neat. Avoid nail decals, black polish or "Elvira"-length nails.

GRUNGY BEARDS. In general, most companies prefer clean-shaven men to, say, ZZ Top. If you just can't part with your facial hair, at least keep it neatly trimmed. (And for gosh sakes check in the mirror after eating that powdered sugar doughnut!)

MICRO-MINISKIRTS. You want to be able to sit without giving a peep show. This cutesy little item may be a staple in a Britney Spears video, but at ABC Accounting Inc., it may go too far in illustrating your bottom line.

PLUNGING NECKLINES. Some of the lawyers on TV can't seem to get through a case without them. However, your office is not trying to garner audience ratings. So button up or wear a tank or camisole under that shirt to conceal the cleavage.

ATHLETIC SOCKS WITH DRESS SHOES. Men, the devil's in the details. People notice these things!

BODY PIERCINGS. Studies show that most people view body jewelry as unprofessional and that people with multiple pierced body parts are less likely to be hired or promoted.

BARE MIDRIFF. Make sure there is at least one inch of room between body and fabric and that your shirt is long enough to conceal your midriff. Let your clothes show off your good taste—not your six-pack abs.

LOW-RISE PANTS. "Plumber's crack" is not acceptable anywhere. Period.

MEN'S CHEST HAIR. Exposing excess chest hair went out of style with leisure suits. Men, you may want to button your shirt an extra button before your clients begin expecting you to ask them what their sign is.

SEE-THROUGH SHIRTS. If you want people to pay attention to what they can learn from your presentation instead of what they see through your shirt, wear a suit coat over or a T-shirt or camisole underneath sheerer fabrics.

OPEN-BACK TOPS AND DRESSES. These may work in the ball-room, but not in the conference room. Slip on a sweater or jacket and go from overexposed to professionally composed.

FLIP-FLOPS. These are appropriate for vacations and lounging, not daily office tasks. If you have problems with your feet, try clogs or even open-toed shoes.

FUNKY FEET. Make sure your feet are presentable. If your toes will be visible, make sure they look good by getting a pedicure. On the day you plan to expose your toes, apply a smoothing moisturizer and a fresh coat of nail polish before leaving the house. Men should wear a conservative slip-on shoe. Socks are optional.

Still fuzzy on how you should dress? Here are some easy-to-follow dos and don'ts:

DO carefully review your company's dress code policy and adhere to it.

DON'T go overboard with trendy styles. Experts say that business casual is a classic style of dress that is crisp and neat.

DO choose clothing that would be appropriate in the event you run into your company's CEO or are invited to sit in on a high-level meeting.

DO make sure clothes fit properly. There's no worse combination than clothes that are too tight when the temperature outside is too warm.

DON'T abuse the relaxed dress code. If you're working out after work, don't wear your sweats to the office. Instead, head to the washroom at quitting time and change your clothes.

DO wear minimal fragrance. It's very uncomfortable for those that must work in proximity to you to endure the constant smell of too much perfume or aftershave. Warm, moist air sometimes makes fragrances overbearing.

Here's what it boils down to: If you have any doubt whether something you have on is appropriate—go back and change.

Chapter 10

PLAYING NICE WITH CO-WORKERS

There's (at least) one annoying co-worker in every office. Whether it's the chatty-Cathy, smelly-Steven, tag-along-Tammy, or just "that guy," difficult co-workers (unfortunately) are the standard in the workplace—not the exception.

Most difficult co-workers are oblivious to their nightmare behavior. Avoiding them is out of the question. If you do make a comment, they stare at you like you're from the moon. Your feelings have been building up for months—maybe even years—and it's time to do something about it. You can either pull your hair out over their obnoxious behaviors, or you can deal with them accordingly.

I. IT'S NOT YOU, IT'S THEM

Like any social situation, a professional environment is bound to have its good and bad apples. There is no rule that says that once you find a job, you will enjoy working with each of your co-workers. In fact, you are bound to run into a colleague who irritates or even offends you. In these situations, it often becomes your responsibility to maintain a professional attitude. Here are some common types of "nightmare co-workers" and tips on how to keep your reputation intact, no matter what.

THE OFFICE GOSSIP—Most offices have one person with a direct connection to the company grapevine. This person has the "scoop" all the time and is not afraid to share it. While it can be fun to be in on the office news for a while, it is best to be cautious when presented with office gossip. The majority of gossip is false and hurtful. If you keep information to yourself instead of passing it on, your co-workers will come to see you as reliable and trustworthy. In addition, deciding not to spread gossip is one of the best ways to keep yourself from eventually becoming the subject.

THE CONSTANT COMPLAINER—Misery loves company, and some individuals are just not happy in any situation. These employees are not afraid to complain, and do it often and vocally. But in an office environment, negativity often means lower productivity and company morale. Complainers typically seek out others who will share their grief. Your best bet is to listen respectfully if someone approaches you to vent, but not to join in. Sooner or later, the complainer will stop using you as a sounding board and you will not have to risk being labeled a negative employee.

THE NOSY NEIGHBOR—Many workplaces are set up in an open environment, with employees situated in cubes rather than in offices. This layout is great for employees who love to learn as much as possible about co-workers' professional and personal lives. If you are faced with a colleague who always knows what is going on in your life, you might want to be more discreet at work. This means keeping personal calls to a minimum, or utilizing a conference room to handle personal business. If your nosy neighbor has truly crossed the line, talk to your manager about the situation.

The company may be able to make adjustments in the office layout to provide you with more privacy.

THE OFFICE THIEF—The office thief typically is not known for stealing pens and pencils, but for stealing credit and ideas. You may find that an idea you brought up casually is later presented formally by this individual, with no reference to your input. Unfortunately, you won't do yourself much good by yelling "that was my idea!" Steer clear of this person, particularly when it comes to brainstorming or sharing ideas and materials. Be professional, but also be guarded in your interactions with the office thief.

THE ALL-AROUND UNPLEASANT CO-WORKER—While some individuals in the office cause problems without being blatantly offensive, this individual is downright nasty— rude, arrogant, condescending and just not enjoyable to be around. There are a couple of tips for dealing with this co-worker. The first is realizing that you never know the whole story. This person might have something going on in his or her life that is causing the negativity. Try having an open conversation— privately, of course—to discuss the interactions between the two of you, but be careful about how you approach the conversation. You want to be seen as supportive and open, rather than accusing. Next, talk to your manager or human resources rep about the situation. It never hurts to document issues, and you may be able to decrease the amount of interaction you have with this individual.

WHEN YOUR JOB LITERALLY STINKS

There's not much worse than being a victim of another person's odor . . . like the colleague who believes there's no such thing as too much eau de cologne and the officemate whose daily announcements that his "dogs are barking" as he kicks off his loafers have put a dark, putrid cloud over 3 p.m.

Unfortunately you're not immune to it at work. Some of the most common smells about which office workers complain:

- Bad breath
- Burned popcorn
- Cigarette smoke
- Foods with overpowering smells like tuna, garlic or onion
- Decaying or moldy leftovers
- Body odor
- Flatulence

For everyone's sake, try keeping these to a minimum.

II. DEALING WITH OFFICE SCOUNDRELS

The Chicago Bears have the Green Bay Packers, Alexander Hamilton had Aaron Burr, and Betty had Veronica. From sports to politics to pop culture, rivalries exist everywhere there's the potential for competition, and the workplace is no exception.

Rivalry between colleagues isn't rare. Oftentimes, it's harmless and could even be a healthy morale booster. Whether you covet the boss's attention or are vying for that promotion, you're all probably trying to stand out from the crowd, a task that requires working that much harder and being that much more productive to get a leg up. But when a colleague stops playing fair and starts playing dirty, the "competition" can quickly go from exciting to excruciating.

According to the Bureau of Labor Statistics, more than a million acts of workplace violence are reported each year. Most injuries sustained were from incidents that involved punching, hitting, kicking and biting. A number of altercations involved superiors and subordinates. Of course, this is on the extreme end of troublesome.

If you're suffering at work, you've got company. From the financial analyst who was coerced into buying kitchen products from his supervisor's wife, to the senior vice president who ordered his marketing director to run a promotion, then made her a scapegoat when it back-fired, the abuses some bosses heap on their underlings can push their workers beyond the brink.

> **TMI! WHAT NOT TO SHARE OR DISCUSS WITH YOUR CO-WORKERS: NEGATIVE VIEWS OF COLLEAGUES**
> If you don't agree with a co-worker's lifestyle, wardrobe or professional abilities, confront that person privately or keep it to yourself. The workplace is not the venue for controversy.

The wrong way

Put-upon employees have exacted revenge (as told to CareerBuilder editors) through the following ill-advised (yet apparently satisfying) means:

- Had subscriptions to fetish magazines sent to the office in the boss's name.

- Stole the boss's clothes out of his locker while he was taking a shower at the corporate fitness center.

- Got into the boss's e-mail, found a message she had written about what a dork the president of the company is and sent it to everyone in the office . . . including the president.

- A woman who was tired of her manager taking credit for her ideas (and aware he couldn't tell a good idea from a bad one) let her boss steal several great ideas, then slipped in five that were so bad the boss was demoted.

- A vice president whose ego was far larger than his own stature was furious when he found out days later that staff members changed his office caller ID to appear as Lord Farquaad, the four-foot tall evil ruler from the movie *Shrek*.

- A group of direct reports decided to give their cheapskate boss his comeuppance by mocking up a $500 gift certificate to an expensive restaurant and sending it with a letter saying he was the winner of a promotional event. He invited friends, ran up a $600 bill and then was told the restaurant would not accept the fake certificate.

- Placed a pair of pants and shoes inside the only toilet stall in a men's room to make it appear someone was using the stall. It sat there for hours until someone called security to check if the person had died.

- Sent a fake love note to a co-worker from another co-worker.

- Called the electric company, used a co-worker's name (and personal information) and said he was moving so the electricity got turned off at the co-worker's house.

- Paged a co-worker over the loudspeaker claiming the CEO was looking for him. The worker went into the CEO's office and the CEO didn't know who he was or why he was there.

- Put a "house for sale" ad in the newspaper regarding a co-worker's home.

(We won't get into some of the other ways employees have gotten even, but let's just say, if you're a rotten manager, you might want to get your own coffee!)

The right way

The best bet is to face the problem head-on and calmly confront the co-worker. Backstabbing co-workers operate under the assumption that no one will challenge them, so they usually back down when someone actually does.

Here are dos and don'ts to follow when confronting your workplace rival:

- **DON'T** be afraid to confront your co-worker directly.

- **DO** confront the person face-to-face rather than try to conduct a discussion via e-mail. E-mails can be used against you or may be misinterpreted.

- **DON'T** make the discussion personal. Keep it short and limited to real workplace issues.

- **DO** use neutral language to calmly discuss the behaviors that are troubling you, the effect the conflict is having on your work and a suggested resolution.

- **DON'T** assume that they will ever change on their own. They usually don't.

- **DO** pick your battles wisely.

If confrontation doesn't work, keep track of everything you are working on. Back up things by saving e-mails, copying other co-workers involved and including others in conversations. Don't stoop to the bully's level—you could wind up damaging your reputation in the process. You can also contact human resources to report the offending behavior, request a transfer to another area or enlist the services of a human resources representative or corporate ombudsman to meet with the two of you to help resolve your differences.

If the person you're confronting is your boss

Since taking these measures will likely force your hand, before doing anything, prepare your résumé, network and have an action plan for your job search.

Of course the ultimate revenge is to rise above your boss. Three years after being let go for not having "enough presence," one account executive found herself in the same executive MBA program with the woman who had fired her. Not only had she gone on to a better job, but she got the satisfaction of watching the professor routinely chastise her former superior!

TMI! WHAT NOT TO SHARE OR DISCUSS WITH YOUR CO-WORKERS: OFF-COLOR OR RACIALLY CHARGED COMMENTS

You may assume your co-worker wouldn't be offended or would think something is funny, but you might be wrong. Never take that risk. Furthermore, even if you know for certain your colleague wouldn't mind your comment, don't talk about it at work. Others can easily overhear.

III. USING HAPPY HOUR TO GET AHEAD

At 5 p.m. on Fridays, many a local bar is transformed into an office hangout as workers beeline from their cubes to their booths to relax and swap stories over Heinekens and mozzarella sticks. In fact, 24 percent of co-workers told CareerBuilder.com they go to happy hour at least once a month.

The benefits of happy hours can go way beyond 50-cent tacos and martini specials. After-hours socializing can help boost worker camaraderie and advance workers' careers—and experts recommend that everyone attend once in awhile.

Why you should make the effort

Showing up for office social functions—even occasionally—signals you're a team player and helps you control your reputation at work. This can mean a happy hour after work or a piece of birthday cake in a conference room.

If you constantly turn down invitations, your co-workers may take offense and your boss might doubt your commitment to the job. Have you ever heard the phrase "making an appearance"? It's better to show up for half an hour than not show up at all.

> **TMI! WHAT NOT TO SHARE OR DISCUSS WITH YOUR CO-WORKERS: HANGOVERS AND WILD WEEKENDS**
> It's perfectly fine to have fun during the weekend, but don't talk about your wild adventures on Monday. That information can make you look unprofessional and unreliable.

The laid-back happy hour atmosphere also provides a perfect opportunity to bond with co-workers and rub elbows with executives. Sharing some personal information—without going overboard—over relaxed cocktails in an environment outside of the office can go a long way with character and business relationship building.

Plus, people naturally talk about work at happy hours, dishing out valuable clues about your industry. You might be surprised how much you learn. And 14 percent of workers said happy hour helped them get closer to a higher-up and land a better position.

Watch your mouth

Show you really care about what your colleagues have to say. Try to listen 75 percent of the time and talk just 25 percent of the time; it can do wonders for your reputation. When you do talk, never share personal problems, gossip or flirt.

Just because alcohol is served at most happy hours and after-hours parties, that doesn't mean you *have* to drink. But if you choose to skip the alcohol, don't act holier-than-thou or make others uncomfortable. You can drink a soda or a club soda with lime and it doesn't have to be a statement.

If you do decide to drink, don't ever forget you're at an office party or get too tipsy. Adam, a publicist who preferred we not use his last name, recalled one office holiday party where a plastered co-worker polled the female employees to determine who was the sexiest man in the office—and then proceeded to announce the results to the president in front of the mortified winner.

"What I learned from all this is go out and have a good time with colleagues, but pay attention to who you are with and what you say," Adam said. "If you do go out, there is not a requirement that you drink or drink in excess. If you feel yourself losing your inhibitions and feel like you might say something inappropriate, go home. Don't jeopardize your job for a $5 beer."

Try leaving everyone feeling they know you a bit better but that you aren't that different from the way you are at work—which is professional, good-natured, hard-working and respectful, right?

POP QUIZ: What work-related topic do co-workers discuss most at happy hour?

A) The boss
B) Other co-workers
C) Job complaints
D) Office gossip

ANSWER: D. While co-workers do make small talk (79 percent) and talk about family (54 percent) and world events (46 percent), their favorite work-related topic of conversation is office gossip (39 percent). They also like to complain about their jobs (36 percent), chitchat about other co-workers (31 percent) and gab about the boss (18 percent).

IV. WHEN LOVE KNOCKS ON THE CUBICLE WALL

While the office tryst was once viewed as a no-no, society no longer frowns upon a romance that blooms between co-workers. With more time spent on the job, an emphasis on group collaboration and increased socializing with co-workers, today's workplace fosters more personal relationships among employees.

In this day and age, most people spend as much time at work with their colleagues as they do outside of work socializing with friends. Because of this, many individuals turn to the workplace to find romance. This phenomenon is no surprise. We share common experiences with our co-workers, relate to the same ideas and often end up socializing once we have punched the clock at the end of the day.

BY THE NUMBERS: LOVE

Four-in-ten (40 percent) workers say they have dated a co-worker at some time during their careers, with 20 percent admitting to doing it more than twice, according to CareerBuilder.com data. Close to three-in-ten (29 percent) workers said they went on to marry the person they dated at work.

Comparing age groups, workers aged 55 and older were least likely (34 percent) to say they have dated a co-worker during their careers, while 44 percent of workers aged 35–44 were the most likely to have done so.

Workers aren't just interested in dating their peers. Twenty-seven percent of workers admit they have dated someone with a higher position in their organization; female workers more so than males, at 37 percent and 20 percent, respectively. Ninety-eight percent of workers said their relationship with someone at work did nothing to progress their career.

Studies show 50 to 80 percent of companies do not have written policies on employee dating. Be careful: Approach any office relationship with caution and check your employee manual to see if your company has a stated policy about dating. At the first sign of flirtation, be discreet and think through the consequences if things don't work out.

It probably won't stay a secret

It's critical to remember that people talk. No matter how friendly your co-workers are, or how tight-lipped the object of your affection seems, secrets are almost always spilled, whether accidentally or intentionally. Translation? Say nothing and do nothing that you don't want everyone else to know about.

Dating a co-worker appears to be more accepted in the office these days with 66 percent of workers saying they do not have to keep their romances a secret at work. It is important to remember to always maintain the highest level of professionalism when dating a co-worker and keep any conflicts that may arise outside the office.

Policies on office romance vary from company to company and it's the workers' responsibility to know where their employer stands. It's important to remember that even if both sides are willing participants, office relationships could have repercussions. The survey also revealed that 6 percent of workers said their office romance drove them to leave their job.

If you find yourself romantically involved with a co-worker, here are some things to consider:

Mum's the word

While any secret is hard to keep, it's best to wait a month or so before you share your romantic news publicly. This will give you a chance to see if the relationship is likely to last past the initial lust and may save face if passions fizzle after the first few weeks.

Avoid P.D.A.

While you may be completely comfortable with your relationship, public displays of affection, such as hand-holding, caresses or even flirting can make others uncomfortable.

Watch the lov-e-mail

As we've mentioned before, some companies prohibit the use of company e-mail systems for personal purposes. Others reserve the right to access or disclose electronic messages or files of an employee with good cause, such as suspected employee wrongdoing or concerns of sexually explicit or pornographic content.

Don't talk about fight club

As with any relationship, whether with a co-worker or someone outside the office, it's best not to bring your arguments to work. Workplace conflicts are difficult enough when two colleagues don't get along. Adding the emotions and tensions of a personal relationship to the mix can create upheaval.

Keep things business as usual

Be a team player and readily available to help others. Don't give people a reason to think you are only working with your sweetheart. Do your job efficiently and creatively. You cannot let your work ethic be compromised. If your romance is affecting your work, you may be asked to end your relationship or find another job. You may have to decide between your career and your companion.

Love hurts

Remember that people do break up. Make sure you remain professional and don't burn bridges.

BY THE NUMBERS: OFFICE ROMANCE

Calling all schmoopies, canoodlers and maker-outers. While romance between co-workers is more commonplace than ever, it rarely begins in the actual office. Thirteen percent of workers saying their relationships began when they ran into each other outside of work. Other situations where office romances found their spark included:

- Happy hour—11 percent
- At lunch—11 percent
- Working after-hours together—10 percent
- Love at first sight—10 percent
- Company office party—2 percent

Chapter 11

WHO'S THE BOSS?

Whether you have the world's best boss or the boss from hell, everyone needs to know the basics of boss-employee relations. Your boss determines your raises, your promotions and your demotions, and they're based on two things: your rapport and performance. We'll tell you how to maximize your opportunities in both facets.

I. IMPRESS THE BOSS

Hollywood is filled with bosses we love to hate: tyrannical Miranda Priestly in *The Devil Wears Prada*, money-hungry Montgomery Burns in *The Simpsons* and egotistical Jack Donaghy in *30 Rock*. And they all have employees dying to get in their good favor.

The same is true in real life. Love 'em or hate 'em, we all want to impress 'em. Whether you're vying for a promotion or just want to show you're a superstar, here's how to show you're star material.

KNOW THE MISSION. Align yourself with your boss's and the company's goals and values. Make your boss's priorities your priorities.

UNDERSTAND HOW YOU'LL BE EVALUATED. Know precisely the skills, behaviors and accomplishments on which you will be judged and rewarded. Focus on them like a laser.

BE DEPENDABLE. Do what you say you're going to do. Better yet, under-promise and over-deliver.

PROJECT POSITIVE ENERGY. Don't be the one to whine or criticize the boss or company direction. Be a motivator: the person everyone wants to be around.

MAKE YOUR BOSS LOOK GOOD. Finish your work on time and with a high level of professionalism. Bring your boss ideas that will help him and the department and offer to take charge and implement them.

OWN UP. Take responsibility for your mistakes by focusing on what you've learned rather than what you've done wrong. For example, "I think this project could have been better if we'd gotten the group's buy-in early on," or "Next time I would talk more with the end users up-front . . ."

BE ORGANIZED. Plan your next day before you leave work. Rank your tasks by urgency and importance and make a point of doing at least the top two items on your list.

BE PUNCTUAL. Arriving for work or meetings on time (even early) shows you're enthusiastic, dependable and able to manage your life effectively.

BE RESOURCEFUL. Don't run to the boss with every question you have or setback you encounter. Think things through first. If you must report a problem to the boss, develop possible solutions to present.

BROADEN YOUR HORIZONS. Take advantage of company-sponsored training courses and volunteer for projects in areas outside your everyday expertise.

STAY INFORMED. Keep abreast of industry and company trends by reading trade journals and attending professional association events.

BE TECH-Y. Stay current with technological, legal and knowledge advances in your area. Upgrade your skills and learn new ones.

BE COURTEOUS. Show respect and loyalty to your boss and speak well of her to others. (At the very least don't bad-mouth her to anyone.)

TRUE STORIES OF LOUSY BOSSES—NOT-SO-SMOOTH CRIMINALS

I once worked at a company where the two owners were, shall we say, somewhat unstable. Strange, contradictory orders would suddenly arrive. Temper tantrums would be thrown for no apparent reason. People would get praise and promotions based on mysterious accomplishments. Games were played with people's minds and emotions. It was a bizarre and somewhat frightening place to work and I got out as soon as I could get a better job.

Years later, I learned that one of the bosses was in a hospital for the criminally insane, while the other was serving time in prison for fraud and stock manipulation. The sad thing was, I was not even a bit surprised. . .

— Jason, Toronto, Ont.

(All names have been changed)

BE FLEXIBLE. Change is inevitable. Companies need people who can adapt and go with the flow.

TAKE CARE OF YOUR HEALTH. When you're run-down, productivity and ambition suffer—as does your image.

LEAVE YOUR PERSONAL LIFE AT THE DOOR. Using your co-workers as therapists not only hurts productivity; it damages your credibility and can contaminate your work relationships (even if people seem sympathetic).

GO BEYOND THE CALL OF DUTY. Take on added challenges, put in extra hours, and never use the phrase, "That's not in my job description."

BE A TEAM PLAYER. Show your boss and co-workers you have their best interests at heart by being empathetic and offering to help out when they need it.

TAKE A BREAK NOW AND THEN. A clear head and balanced life can give you energy and perspective.

LOOK AND ACT PROMOTABLE. Don't let anyone think you work because you have to. A boss is more likely to promote and give a raise to a committed and engaged employee than one who just checks in and checks out.

TRUE STORIES OF LOUSY BOSSES— INSURANCE? WHAT INSURANCE?

Several years ago, I worked for a small communications agency in the city. While I regularly rode my bike to work, one day on my way in, I was hit by a car. In shock from the accident and on autopilot, I ended up at work where I started to realize what had happened.

I called a friend who worked at the hospital and he insisted he come pick me up, and that I needed to make sure I was OK. I agreed and told my boss what happened, and that my friend was going to pick me up and take me to the hospital. As I was leaving, my boss said, "Make sure she's back this afternoon."...

Even more shocking than his insensitivity to my accident (and my health) was the hospital bill. While I had given the hospital my insurance card at check-in, I was billed for the full amount of the X-rays and doctor time. When I called the insurance company to find out why, the number on the card was incorrect. I asked my boss about it and he gave me a new number. After going around and around with him and the insurance company, my boss eventually confessed he had lied: We never had health insurance!

— Kevin, Portland, Ore.

II. THINGS YOU SHOULD NEVER SAY TO THE BOSS

Somewhere between winning the lottery and hearing your name called on *The Price is Right* is that other common fantasy: Telling off your boss. While informing your supervisor what he or she can really do with that quarterly report is tempting, you'd like to keep your job.

Still, you may not be aware of how other things you say to your boss can make you come across as lazy, disrespectful or careless, sabotaging your chances of getting a promotion, a raise or a better job later on. Below are the phrases hiring managers say they most hate to hear and why.

"I REALLY NEED TO TALK TO YOU, IT'S IMPORTANT." In today's fast-paced workplace, managers don't have time to personally attend to every little need. If you have to talk to your boss about something important, explain what it's regarding first.

"I DON'T NEED ANYONE TO TEACH ME." Be careful here. It's one thing to already know how to perform a job; it's another (irritating) thing to think you already know all there is to learn.

"I DON'T UNDERSTAND." On the other hand, while a little on-the-job training is standard, someone who continually needs instructions on how to perform a certain task can be, in a manager's eyes, more effort than he or she is worth.

"COULD YOU REPEAT THAT?" A forgivable offense if it's a one-time occurrence, but continually asking your manager to repeat information indicates you don't care about or respect what he or she has to say.

"I JUST NEVER GOT AROUND TO IT." Sometimes not following through can be a greater offense than saying the wrong thing. An employee who is unreliable will be remembered when it comes time for evaluations or promotions—in a bad way.

"THAT'S NOT IN MY JOB DESCRIPTION." Unless the task your manager is asking you to perform has nothing to do with the actual workplace, you should keep this thought to yourself. Everyone needs to pitch in, which sometimes means performing work that may be a departure from your day-to-day duties.

TRUE STORIES OF LOUSY BOSSES— EARPLUGS OPTIONAL

At a previous position, my boss was notoriously unprofessional, making him infamous throughout the organization. In addition to partaking in the community pretzel bin while suffering from a finger fungus and perspiring so profusely that he would be sporting two-foot-long sweat stains before 9 a.m., he believed his office was a personal recording studio.

You name it—from Van Halen to Avril Lavigne—he was bolting it out at a high-decibel level all day. But the day I heard Jessica Simpson was the day I knew it was leave my job or lose my sanity. Nothing beats a middle-aged, overweight man with slicked-back hair singing: "Nothin' but a T-shirt on . . . never felt so beautiful, baby as I do now . . . now that I'm with you."

— Aimee, Fort Lauderdale, Fla.

"DON'T BLAME ME—IT'S NOT MY FAULT." One thing that's sure to tick off your boss is trying to cover up a mistake by blaming someone else. This behavior proves to your boss that you're not only unreliable, but deceptive as well.

"CAN YOU TELL SO-AND-SO TO SHUT OFF THAT ANNOYING MUSIC?" It's not up to the boss to solve your personal problems. If you can't resolve a problem with a co-worker on your own, you can ask your boss for advice, but don't expect a response to whining and complaining.

"YEAH, RIGHT. I HAVE A FAMILY. I'M GOING HOME." True, the workday for most officially ends at 5 p.m., but a little overtime work every once in a while is standard in many workplaces. Make sure you understand your company's policy on overtime before you speak up.

"GET YOURSELF A SERVANT." Even if you're leaving, be careful where you burn your bridges. A former boss can be a good professional reference for future positions, so you may regret leaving on such bitter terms later on.

TRUE STORIES OF LOUSY BOSSES—WANTED: GOOD COOK WITH A VALID DRIVER'S LICENSE

I decided to be my own boss after a myriad bad bosses. Here are a few examples:

Boss No. 1: Wanted me to schedule his colonoscopy and drive him to his appointment. He also made cleaning his iguana tank a requirement.

Boss No. 2: Suggested I take cooking lessons so I could make his lunch.

Boss No. 3: Wanted me to negotiate with his wife over their "property." (I was a mediator at the time.) He thought I could show up for a meeting with his wife and her attorney in order to get him everything he wanted without hiring an attorney.

Boss No. 4: I was a backup singer for an infamous '60s pop star. He would expect me to drive him to the grocery store anywhere from 1 to 3 a.m. in order for him to purchase makeup, Lysol and other weird items—only to be left in the hotel room. He didn't drive, and my position was to be chauffeur in addition to performing with him as a singer. I was really creeped out by this—many people thought I was his girlfriend or his former wife . . . Yuck! After that experience, I went for the regimentation of law school!

— Mary, Santa Clara, Calif.

III. QUESTIONS YOU SHOULD ASK THE BOSS

You probably have a list of questions you'd ask your boss if given the chance, like:

"You really paid someone for that haircut?"

"Must your lunch always include garlic?"

"How did someone as nice as you end up marrying someone so unpleasant?"

If you still have your job, you've already made the wise decision to keep those questions to yourself. Unfortunately employees have a tendency to keep *all* questions to themselves, even when speaking up can help their careers. Asking the right questions in the workplace is just as important as asking them in an interview. Questions about the broader organization's goals and priorities, your role and feedback on your performance tell your boss you are focused on a career with the organization, not just a job.

So whether you've kept quiet because you're afraid of embarrassing yourself or you don't think your questions mean much, you should start speaking up. Here are nine questions to ask your boss that can help your career. (Just don't ask them all at once—your boss is probably a busy person.)

"How do you measure success?"

Employees often forget that their performances are graded in some form or another. To understand how your work is evaluated, you should be speaking the same language as your boss. Is your manager just concerned about the numbers or is your role in achieving those numbers important, too? Base your future work on your boss's priorities.

"What areas do I need to develop to advance my career?"

This shows your boss that you are interested in directing a path for your career and not just riding the wave. If you can articulate what your career goals are, your boss can tell you what experience you need to gain before you can move up the ladder.

"What strengths do I have that will help my career?"

Don't be so focused on looking for your weaknesses that you forget to ask about your strong points. You might think you know what your strengths and weaknesses are, but your boss could have a different opinion. You're not fishing for compliments here. You're just demonstrating your desire to steer your career.

"How often are performance evaluations conducted and who is in charge of them?"

If you didn't ask this in your interview, you should ask it now. Understanding the mechanics of your job should be a top priority at all times. Make sure you know if you have quarterly or annual goals to aim for and how they impact your daily tasks.

"What are the options for growth within the organization?"

This is another question that should be asked in the interview, but also after you've made your mark. Company structures change all the time and you should know what opportunities are open to you if you want to advance. Once you know what your options are, you can decide what your next move is, whether it's aiming for a new position or looking for a job with a better future.

"Do I understand this correctly?"

When you have a project that has many components or a new set of guidelines, be certain you have a grasp on what your task is. Tackling an assignment without knowing you're on the right path leaves the opportunity for a rude awakening on the due date. Check in with your boss to ensure you understand everything the way it was intended.

Caution: Use restraint when asking this question. No boss wants to repeat himself or herself ad nauseam.

"What can I do to help you?"

This is a simple, yet often forgotten question. Even if you can't help, your boss will take note of your offer. Show your boss you're not only interested in your career success, but his or hers also, and you'll stand out.

"What is the most important priority we need to focus on?"

This question often goes unasked because employees fear appearing incompetent. Really, it shows concern about your responsibilities and your team's goals. When you have several ongoing projects and your boss adds more to your workload, knowing how to prioritize grows difficult.

"Can I take on this task?"

Rather than let your career meander, look for opportunities to prove you have initiative and leadership skills. Find ways to build experience and gain skills that you currently lack.

IV. STICKY SITUATIONS

If you're more excited that your boss is out sick with the flu than you are about your new raise, you're in good company.

In workplaces throughout the country, difficult bosses are ruining morale and making life just downright unpleasant. Whether they refuse to give you time off or they expect you to be their mother, bad bosses can put you in an awkward position.

Believe it or not, your boss might not realize his demands are making you miserable, so communication is crucial. A direct approach will save time and anxiety for both you and your boss. You can't resolve anything if you keep your concerns to yourself. Just letting him know how you feel could solve your problems.

Here are eight (unfortunately) common workplace situations that bosses often put employees in and advice on how you should handle them:

STICKY SITUATION NO. 1: You are not a personal assistant, but your boss continually asks you to pick up her dry cleaning.

HOW TO DEAL: Try talking to your boss in a diplomatic manner, stressing the pending work you have to prioritize. Expressing your desire to become more involved with important, work-related projects should gently remind your boss that you were not hired to organize her personal life.

Of course, if your boss's demands are an indication of a deep-seated and unalterable power struggle, you'll need to decide if you're willing to accept that her requests are part and parcel of your workload—whether or not they're in the job description.

STICKY SITUATION NO. 2: Your boss frequently loses his temper and yells at you in front of your co-workers.

HOW TO DEAL: Again, be open with your boss. Allowing your emotions to surface will only intensify matters, so it's best to be calm and collected when you enter this conversation. Ask your boss to identify examples of things you do that trigger his temper so you can figure out if they are truly mistakes. If a discussion does not lead to change, you'll need to decide if you want to join your co-workers' code of silence, or voice your concerns to a supervisor.

STICKY SITUATION NO. 3: While your boss kicks back in her office making personal calls, you're doing both your job and hers. When the time comes to present projects to senior management, your boss takes credit for your hard work.

HOW TO DEAL: You can still get credit for your work. Casually mention your involvement during meetings with senior management. You might also consider keeping leaders informed of the work you've done by copying them on memos or e-mails over the course of a project. (This does not mean CC-ing everyone all the time!)

STICKY SITUATION NO. 4: Your boss subtly hits on you, but you know he would deny his actions if you mentioned they were upsetting you.

HOW TO DEAL: As discussed earlier, office romance is not so taboo anymore. BUT, when it involves the boss, it can cross the line. Mention you are in a relationship. If that doesn't work, try explaining to your boss that his or her behavior has made you uncomfortable. If your boss's conduct continues, you should make a written account of each incident as it occurs, discuss the situation with your boss's supervisor, and consider making a formal complaint with human resources.

STICKY SITUATION NO. 5: Your human resources department encourages employees to use their vacation time, but your boss grumbles angrily every time you ask to take time off.

HOW TO DEAL: A frank conversation with your boss might reveal that she feels your vacation requests coincide with the company's busiest and most demanding periods. Give your boss notice as soon as you might know of any plans for time off so you can all plan accordingly.

STICKY SITUATION NO. 6: You receive your annual bonus and are distressed to find it's significantly lower than your boss has verbally promised.

HOW TO DEAL: There might have been a misunderstanding; discuss the matter with your boss before jumping to any conclusions. If your boss can provide a reasonable answer—perhaps the company is going through difficult times and bonuses are lower than expected across the board—it might be best to overlook the discrepancy. But if you still feel you are owed a larger bonus, you will need to decide whether it's worth rocking the boat before going above your boss's head to resolve the matter.

STICKY SITUATION NO. 7: Your boss continually solicits your advice regarding his personal problems.

HOW TO DEAL: Look first at your own actions to make sure you haven't unwittingly implied to your boss that you're an available confidante. If your behavior isn't what needs altering, suggest a more appropriate person for your boss to take his problems to, such as a family member or friend.

STICKY SITUATION NO. 8: You suspect your boss of unethical and potentially illegal business practices.

HOW TO DEAL: This is one situation where you probably don't want to confront your boss directly. Document any evidence you find before informing the company of your boss's actions. Discuss your suspicions and evidence with HR in a diplomatic and timely manner.

TRUE STORIES OF LOUSY BOSSES— STICKY SITUATION

I worked for a small PR firm a few years ago. . . . One day I was working in my office and inadvertently spilled a can of soda in my lap. I was soaked right down to my underwear. When I told my direct boss—a young woman—what had happened, and that I was going to run home to change, she told me no and suggested that I remove the pants and drape them over the heater. She wanted me to basically sit in my office in my underwear in the middle of winter.

The worst part is, I actually did it! Let's just say when I gave notice there a few months later, it was the best decision I made in my life!

—Joanie, Levittown, N.Y.

Chapter 12

MOVING ON UP

So you managed to survive your first year or so on the job and the inevitable happens—your annual review. Some employers have a formal review process, some barely remember to do them at all. But the same thing happens: You and your boss review your successes and failures, strengths and weaknesses, where you go from here and, hopefully, you get a raise. But, just like an interview, we can't stress the importance of preparation.

I. PERFORMANCE REVIEWS

There's one certainty in life beyond death and taxes for employees—it's the dreaded performance review. For some people, approaching an annual performance review is something that can bring about all of the classic symptoms of stress: sweaty palms, dry mouth, butterflies in the stomach and nervous twitches. These employees are usually unprepared for reviews and have no idea what they are going to hear. Thus, sitting through a review is like waiting for the ax to fall. They go in, hold their breath and hope to come out with some shred of dignity intact.

Others, however, learn to take charge of their performance reviews and find that the experience is helpful, not horrifying. A good annual review should give you the opportunity to discuss your career path, review your accomplishments, and pinpoint ways to make sure you are achieving all you can at your company.

If you have a review in your future, there is one word to keep in mind: preparation. Thinking ahead will ensure you are not surprised by your company's opinion of you and you get everything you can out of the review. Need some help getting ready?

Here are a few ways to make sure you go into your review with all of the tools you need.

Think like a historian

It is important in your review to show evidence of your accomplishments throughout that past year. Don't expect your boss to remember these achievements for you. Think back to the previous months. What have you done well? What goals have you met? What projects have you tackled? Make a list of your achievements and ways in which you have excelled. Then, like any good historian, start finding evidence to back up your accomplishments. If you have received letters from satisfied customers, pull those out of your files. Gather up those reports that show how you increased your division's sales by 25 percent over the year. Put together copies of publications you designed that received positive feedback. The key is building a cache of positive "press" to demonstrate your worth.

Compile a cheat sheet

Once you have come up with your strengths and accomplishments, put them all down on paper. Make a table that has all of your goals for the previous year on one side, and how you met those goals on the other side. List your major strengths and achievements. Prepare some brief "talking points" for yourself to keep you focused in your meeting. This will ensure that you don't forget to mention key points about your performance in the past year, and will demonstrate to your boss that you are professional and willing to go the extra mile to prepare.

Pinpoint your weaknesses

Everyone has room for improvement, and it is important to look at your review as an opportunity to make yourself better. Don't let your boss blindside you with criticisms you have never considered. Think about your performance seriously and try to come up with areas you can improve. If you have dropped the ball in the past year, think about those situations and figure out how you could have avoided them. Doing this will ensure that you can keep your cool and professionalism during your review, even when your efforts are criticized.

Scramble if you need to

Do you have projects that have not been finished? Is there anything you can do at the last minute to make yourself look better? If so, get moving. While it is never great to have to play catch up, putting in the effort before your review will at least show that you have taken the time to get the job done. Scrambling to complete unfinished tasks at the last minute is still better than facing your boss with a long list of "to-do" items left unchecked. When it comes to performance reviews, the bottom line is you should never be surprised by what you hear. If you take some time to prepare and think clearly about the year that has passed, you will be ready for anything that comes your way.

BY THE NUMBERS
Nearly 30 percent of workers think they can do their boss's job better.

II. SURVIVING A BAD REVIEW

Receiving a glowing appraisal is easy. It can do wonders for your morale and can be a great motivator. Receiving a poor review, on the other hand, can leave you dejected and frustrated. The trick is learning how to turn a less-than-stellar review into a valuable learning experience:

TAKE THE CRITICISM MATURELY AND PROFESSIONALLY. Let's face it—it is not easy to be criticized in any situation. But rather than being offended, learn from it. Keep your emotions in check and resist the urge to be defensive.

ASK FOR SPECIFICS. The best way to improve your performance is if you know what you are doing wrong. Ask your manager to spell out exactly where you are lacking so you can make improvements. If he or she simply says that you "don't seem to be motivated" in the office, respectfully ask for examples of where and when you have fallen short. This will help you see things from your manager's perspective.

UNDERSTAND EXPECTATIONS. Sometimes, being a star at work is all about expectations. You need to understand your manager's expectations to meet them. Ask your manager to give you examples of accomplishments or behaviors that are required to earn a better evaluation.

SET CLEAR AND ATTAINABLE GOALS. The best way to show that you are improving is to set goals and meet those goals. With your supervisor's help develop a list of short- and long-term goals that go along with the areas in your review. This will demonstrate that you are committed to improvement and will give you a road map to follow.

DON'T GO IT ALONE. If you find that you need assistance, ask for it. Maybe you just haven't gotten the hang of the new accounting system or are having troubles managing a certain client. If you don't step up and ask for help, your work—and your career—will continue to suffer.

MEET REGULARLY. If the only time you sit down with your boss is at your annual review, it may be difficult for you to improve much in the workplace. You need to build a relationship with your manager that provides you with ongoing support and feedback. If necessary, set up meetings every few weeks to talk about your goals and discuss your progress.

KEEP A RECORD. The workplace has a short memory and a performance review is normally conducted just once a year. That's why it is important for you to keep a file of your accomplishments throughout the year. Share these with your supervisor as he prepares your performance appraisal to remind him of your achievements.

III. PITFALLS TO AVOID WHEN ASKING FOR A RAISE

Usually right around performance review time, the subject of money is on your mind. You've been doing a good job, putting in your time. Hey, you've even stayed past 5 p.m. a few times. You're going to ask for a raise. What's the worst that can happen?

Well, a few things, actually. It could backfire. You could get demoted, or worse, fired, if you don't ask for a raise in the proper way.

We're not trying to scare you (much), but asking for a raise requires preparation, skill and timing. Many employees take this issue lightly, assuming raises are based on work ethic, time commitments and even personal issues. (Trust us, telling your boss you're saving for a trip to Europe will NOT convince her to give you a raise.)

Employees are almost never aware of other things that come into play when it comes to salary: workplace dynamics, co-workers' qualifications and how others are paid.

To build your case for a raise, try putting a plan in place when you're first hired. If achieved in a timely fashion, you get a raise and repeat the process. People often don't set a path for progression but are shocked when they are passed up for a raise or promotion.

Here are some insider tips to asking for a raise or a promotion the right way:

Avoid telling your employer you hope she'll say yes

INSTEAD: Start by inviting your boss to say no. Tell her you're comfortable with a no answer and you want her to be comfortable to say no. This puts her at ease and clears the air.

Avoid being emotional

INSTEAD: Turn your mind into a blank slate. Have no expectations, hopes or fears. Above all, overcome all neediness, the No. 1 deal-killer. Not *needing* this raise or promotion gives you power.

Avoid going into the meeting unprepared

INSTEAD: Research what people in your position get paid. Find out what obstacles stand in your way. Has the company just fired employees? Is there new management in the wings? Know all the issues that might keep your boss from giving you a raise. State each problem clearly and ask your boss how these problems might be solved.

Avoid trying to impress your boss

INSTEAD: Let her feel completely at ease with you, and perhaps even a little superior. Never dress to impress, brag or be pretentious.

Avoid giving a presentation

INSTEAD: Talk as little as possible. Ask your employer a lot of questions so you can find out her position, issues, concerns, needs and objectives.

Avoid asking yes or no questions

INSTEAD: Get your employer to spill the beans by beginning all of your questions with an interrogative: who, what, when, where, how or why.

Avoid thinking about the outcome

INSTEAD: Don't think about, hope for or plan on getting the raise. Focus instead on what you can control: your behavior during the negotiation.

Avoid believing that your mission is to get more money

INSTEAD: Your mission and purpose in this conversation is to fulfill your *employer's* business needs and objectives. Every decision you make in the negotiation process should be focused on helping your employer see that giving you a raise or promotion will further *her* business interests.

Avoid presenting your current salary or position as a problem

INSTEAD: Present yourself as the solution. Don't be afraid to give specific examples of challenges you faced and the solutions you provided. Special assignments that fit the employer's vision should be explained and discussed. The more examples you can provide the better.

Avoid giving an ultimatum

INSTEAD: Continue to negotiate with no need. Never threaten or posture with another offer or a take-it-or-leave-it stance. Use a calm, slow voice. State problems clearly and don't be afraid to ask for what you need to solve those problems. The more effective you appear at discussing the problem as you see it, the better.

THE BOTTOM LINE

No matter how perfect your job might be, there will always be some hiccups along the way. From time to time, you'll have battles—big and small—you'll need to fight. Hopefully we've given you the tools to meet them head-on.

If, despite all your efforts, you're doing more complaining than collaborating or stressing out rather than saving the day, perhaps it's time to consider your options.

WHEN YOUR JOB ISN'T WORKING OUT

Here's the situation: You're on a gorgeous beach somewhere with nary a BlackBerry or intern in sight. Two weeks of tropical bliss far, far away from your obnoxious boss, your chatty co-workers and incessant e-mails.

But you know someone's going to say it.

Or you're going to think it.

That whiny, "I don't want to go back to work."

And instead of just a groan (Really. We all do it no matter how much we love our jobs.) you have an intense physical reaction similar to the first time you saw the face-peeling scene in *Poltergeist*. The mere thought of your job—even thousands of miles and several days away—causes feelings of utter horror and a wave of nausea that nearly cause you to upchuck all over your margarita-savoring, coconut-smelling, sleeping-til-noon, blissed-out self.

Sound familiar? OK, this is an extreme situation. But getting violently ill at the thought of work isn't the only sign you need to seek greener pastures.

If you're unsatisfied with any aspect of your job, from the amount of work you're taking on to the way your chair squeaks every time you move, it is up to you to change your situation. For those of you who want to make the leap to a new job but just can't quite seem to take that first step, these tips on networking, contacts, resigning the right way, keeping bridges intact, getting recommendations and more will help get you moving in the right direction on the road to career happiness.

Chapter 13

BURNOUT

If you tend to break out in a cold sweat or experience waves of nausea when you think about work, you might be suffering from job burnout. Consider these statistics:

- In a 2008 CareerBuilder survey, 78 percent of workers said they feel burnout at work.

- The American worker has the least vacation time of any modern, developed society.

- In 2008, 24 percent of workers said they would be checking in with the office while on vacation.

- One-half of workers reported they feel a great deal of stress on the job.

- Forty-four percent of working moms admit to being pre-occupied about work while at home, and one-fourth say they bring home projects at least one day a week.

- Nineteen percent of working moms reported they often or always work weekends.

- Thirty-seven percent of all working dads said they would consider the option of taking a new job with less pay if it offered a better work/life balance.

- Thirty-six percent of working dads reported they bring work home at least one day a week, and 30 percent say they often or always work weekends.

These statistics, taken from CareerBuilder.com surveys of American workers, demonstrate the pressures employees in the United States are under to be available to the office, despite responsibilities—or plans—away from work. All this, coupled with longer work hours and many individuals handling the workloads of two, can easily lead to worker burnout.

I. SIGNS OF JOB BURNOUT . . . AND WHAT TO DO ABOUT IT

If you think burnout on the job is just an excuse used by the weak to get out of responsibilities, think again. Stress and burnout can affect your immune system and has been linked to migraines, digestive disorders, skin diseases, high blood pressure and heart disease. It causes emotional distress as well.

If you've noticed any (or all) of these five warning signs of burnout, it's time to take action before the situation worsens:

Sign No. 1: Your co-workers are walking on eggshells around you

If you find yourself becoming cranky and irritable with co-workers you used to get along with, it may be more than just typical interpersonal dynamics.

Sign No. 2: You come in late and want to leave earlier

You used to wake up in the morning excited for another day, but now every day you dread heading into the office. Once lunch passes you start watching the clock, counting the minutes to the end of the day.

Sign No. 3: Apathy has replaced enthusiasm

You feel no motivation, no sense of accomplishment and have no desire to be challenged. Those who have burnout lose their motivation to perform, as well as their feelings of pride for a job well done.

Sign No. 4: You've lost camaraderie with co-workers

You're no longer interested in the company network. You used to go to lunch, go out for drinks and participate in other company functions but now have no desire for socializing in or out of the office.

Sign No. 5: You're feeling physically sick

You always feel exhausted, have headaches, feel tension in all of your muscles and are having trouble sleeping. These physical signs are common indicators of job stress, and demonstrate that this can turn into a physical problem.

If you are experiencing these symptoms, it's time to make some changes.

- You can start by talking to your boss or someone in your human resources department about how you can confront the problem together by redefining deadlines, delegating or outsourcing a project or two.

- Evaluate your career goals and assess the parts of your job that fit these goals.

- Take a vacation. Even if you don't travel anywhere, schedule some time off and commit that time to you. This is not the time to commit to a big household project. Catch up on sleep, play with your kids and pets, read that book you can't quite seem to get to.

BY THE NUMBERS
One-in-ten workers have forfeited four or more vacation days in a given year because they didn't have time to use them.

II. COPING WITH A JOB YOU HATE

There's just no denying the signs. In fact you don't need any signs at all, you just can't stand your job. But how many of us have the luxury of just up and leaving a lousy job without having another lined up?

Having a job you hate is never an easy thing to deal with, but sometimes you just need to grin and bear it until you have another gig lined up. Whether you're currently stuck because you just have to pay the bills or are holding out for the next great opportunity, here are some ways to get through the day:

SET WEEKLY GOALS FOR YOURSELF. Sometimes it is easier to make it to 5 o'clock when you can keep your eye on the prize. Even if you hate your job now, there is something out there that will make you happy. Make weekly goals to help you find that golden opportunity. One week you might strive to send out five résumés or attend one networking event. Setting these goals will give you something to work toward.

DO ONE THING EACH DAY TO HELP YOU REACH YOUR GOALS. You don't need to cross all your goals off your list every day, but you can chip away daily. When you get up in the morning, set a daily objective for yourself and make sure you achieve it. This will give you a sense of accomplishment and keep you feeling good about your progress.

GIVE YOURSELF "ME TIME" BEFORE WORK. Going into a job you hate will be worse if you get to the office feeling rushed, stressed and frazzled. Set aside some moments of solitude each morning. Develop a positive morning ritual. Treat yourself to a latte, get up early enough to read the paper, or just set your alarm to play upbeat music when you wake up. Improving your mornings can do wonders for the rest of your day.

CREATE A DIVERSION FOR YOURSELF IN THE OFFICE. Does being in your office make you yearn for the outdoors? Are the incessant ringing phones driving you batty? Do something to brighten your mood while you're at work. Take in a tropical picture and use it as your screensaver. Buy yourself a "joke of the day" desk calendar. Plug headphones into your computer or bring your iPod to work. Go out for lunch.

USE YOUR TIME TO DEVELOP YOUR SKILLS. Hating your job doesn't mean you can't learn new skills. Use your time to make yourself a better candidate down the road. If your company offers training courses, take advantage of them. Use downtime to learn something new on your computer. Pick up a management development book and read it at lunch. Turn this job into an opportunity for self-improvement.

BLOW OFF SOME STEAM. Most people have an activity that helps them unwind and get rid of tension. Go for a run after work, go swimming on your lunch hour, or take a nice long walk. Put this activity on your schedule so you will have something to look forward to every day.

TREAT YOURSELF. To make up for your office misery, find little ways of treating yourself. Buy a good book to read. Treat yourself to ice cream. Buy some flowers. Shop for a new interview suit. Plan your next vacation. Find out what makes you feel better inside, no matter what is going on outside.

MAINTAIN YOUR PERFORMANCE. It is important to continue to do your work and do it well, regardless of your current situation. Set personal performance goals. Then use the accomplishments in future interviews.

KEEP YOUR BRIDGES INTACT. It really is a small world, and you never know when you will run into co-workers from your past. Don't burn any bridges at your company because you are unhappy. Maintain your contacts and keep your relationships positive. You might just need a reference or a good word from one of your colleagues in the future.

REALIZE THAT THIS TOO SHALL PASS. Right now, it might seem like you will be stuck in this job forever. Keep your chin up and remind yourself that you are in charge of your destiny. Search internal postings for new positions. Start your search for a new job externally.

Chapter 14

QUITTING TIME?

I. IT'S THAT TIME . . .

"I like what I do. I just don't like where I work." Sound familiar?

From unbearable co-workers to depressing work environments, there are things that can make even the best job a living hell. Here's how you know it's time to look for a new job.

Your co-workers are annoying

They live for themselves and only themselves. They irritate you. They offend you. They have no manners or ethics. And you work with them all. How are you supposed to get any work done when these guys keep getting in the way? They are distracting and impede productivity. Most offices have a Gossip, that one person who has the "scoop" all the time and is not afraid to share it. Misery loves company, and finds it often in the Whiner, who isn't afraid to complain and bellyache. There's the Office Thief who steals your ideas. The Shirker arrives late, leaves early and disappears whenever work is near. The Buck-passer unloads his work onto everyone else and blames others for his mistakes. The Procrastinator delays things until the last possible minute, slowing you down by not having the information you need to meet your deadlines. The Interrupter stops by your cubicle ten times a day to chat about her latest boyfriend despite your ringing telephone and pressing deadlines. Maybe it's time to find some co-workers you fit in with?

The environment is toxic

Everyone experiences job highs and lows, but discontent could also be a sign of a chronically depressing work environment, or even a company in peril. A bad work environment is reflective of the culture of an entire business. Do you work in a less-than-nurturing atmosphere? Is morale constantly low? Have you been complaining for two solid years? It could be an organizational problem that applying feng shui to your cube just won't fix.

You're mentally exhausted by the end of the day

Stress can cause low morale, decreased productivity and apathy toward work. Plus, it can spill into your personal life and even have a negative effect on your health. Today fewer people are taking on more and more work. American workers experience burnout at an alarming rate. According to CareerBuilder data, more than half of workers said they work under a great deal of stress, and 78 percent said they feel burnout on the job. Yes, we all have to pick up some slack and "take one for the team" from time to time. But if there's no end in sight, do yourself and your health a favor and dust off your résumé.

Your boss is a nightmare

Your boss doesn't have license to do just anything just because he or she is the boss. If you have a lousy boss, even the best job in the world can become the worst. Your relationship with your supervisor plays a big role in your overall professional happiness and success. Fighting to have your boss removed or waiting for your boss to change or get fired are rarely successful tactics. If you are working for someone who is always absent, unavailable, self-absorbed or untrustworthy, it's time to look for a better supervisor and a better opportunity.

You're watching the clock . . . every ten minutes

Though you might not like to work, it's even worse when you are bored while you're there. One can only watch so many videos on YouTube or bid on unneeded things on eBay. If you aren't feeling challenged, that's a sign that you need additional responsibilities or a change in roles. And be warned, if you don't have any responsibility or find yourself with nothing to do, management might be trying to phase you out and you might be in danger of losing your job.

You get no respect

Does any of this sound familiar? Your ideas aren't taken seriously; there are no opportunities for advancement; the boss ignores you; co-workers alienate you; you're discouraged from improving skills with a course or seminar; you're passed over for a promotion— again; or you're excluded from key projects and strategizing sessions. So why are you still giving this organization your time, energy and great ideas?

You feel stifled

What kind of quality of life do you have? Is your 40-hour week turning into a 24/7 grind? While salary may seem like the end all and be all, your quality of life determines your overall happiness. How much time you spend on the job, working conditions, supervisors and subordinates can positively and negatively impact your job outlook. If you dread the time you spend at work, it should be a clear indicator that it's time to break free. A job shouldn't stifle you creatively, mentally or physically.

Nobody communicates

Although we live in a world of e-mail, cell phones, instant messages, BlackBerries, Wi-Fi and, yes, even face-to-face conversation, there can still be a complete lack of communication. Whether it's a co-worker who's not returning your voice mail or the CEO not conveying a company's goals and accomplishments, the breakdown of communication can be frustrating and detrimental to your job. It can cost you an account, make you miss a deadline, cause you to lose a client and even get you fired.

You're not valued

Thirty-five percent of workers told CareerBuilder they do not feel appreciated at their organizations. You need to realize that you deserve credit for your successes. Recognition is important, and good companies implement programs to let employees know they are valued. Is your company doing anything to reward your efforts? Do you ever receive bonuses, perks or positive feedback? If your boss has never heard of positive reinforcement verbal or otherwise, find a company that will value your talents.

Figuring out what you don't like about your current situation should give you insight into what you are seeking in future endeavors. If you know what your priorities and preferences are and actively seek them, work can be an enjoyable experience.

II. JOB SEARCHING ON COMPANY TIME

You're told to treat your job search like a full-time job. But when do you have the time to look with a schedule that includes working 50-plus hours a week, going to school, caring for a family, running errands and trying to squeeze in some shut-eye? Simple. You do it at work.

Whether they are scouring job boards, searching company Web sites or monitoring blogs, 11 million people on average look for jobs online every week. One-quarter of workers who use a computer at work admit to searching on company time, according to a survey by staffing company Hudson Highland Group. And, job site traffic spikes on weekdays during lunchtime hours.

But proceed with caution when searching for a job on company time; the key is to keep your current job, and income, until you find a new one. Follow these tips to stay under the radar:

Know the rules

We warned you in chapter seven about how employers monitor employees' technology use on company time. A growing number of employers have established policies on employee Internet use including monitoring employee personal e-mail abuse, personal instant messenger use, operation of personal Web sites on company time, personal postings on corporate blogs and operation of personal blogs on company time.

Play it safe

Use a personal e-mail account when discussing job search–related items and applications. Employers would rather receive correspondence from personal accounts than from competitor addresses anyway—you don't want to send a message to a potential new employer that you conduct job searches on company time.

Don't advertise your search

Don't wear your interview suit to your biz-casual office. Nothing sets off a red flag like wearing a suit to your dressed-down office. So how should you handle the wardrobe dilemma? For both men and women, suit bottoms (i.e., pants, skirts) are always passable for business casual. Bring a shoulder bag/duffle with a jacket in it, and change en route to/from the interview. For women, it is especially easy to wear a casual shell under a suit—once a jacket and stockings are removed, no one will detect an afternoon interviewee. For men, make sure your shirt stands on its own without a tie and you can easily make the switch.

Choose references wisely

Former co-workers are usually the first ones to turn to if you want to keep your search confidential. But current co-workers are really the ideal names to pass along to your potential employer. Put a significant amount of thought into who will keep your confidence at your current job. Oftentimes, people find peers rather than managers to be safer bets. As long as your reference can speak to your work ethic, enthusiasm, drive and accomplishments, you don't need to search high and low for a senior executive to speak on your behalf—go with who knows you best.

Timing is everything

The breakfast interview is an ideal forum. Meetings scheduled at 8 a.m. are often finished in time to arrive at work by 9 a.m. If they run over, any number of reasons can be offered for a delayed arrival, but don't go over the top. "Personal time" for a relaxing respite is still an acceptable reason for taking vacation time. Claiming to be sick runs you the risk of being asked to log on and work from home, or at least to make yourself available. The best maneuvers are those when an interview can be tacked on to other pre-planned time off (long weekends, etc.) or nonwork hours.

Never stop giving your all at work

Job seekers can experience intense paranoia at work. If you devote yourself fully to what you're doing in the hours you're there (and job search with a vengeance in the hours when you're not), you'll continue to get the praise and recognition to keep you on track at your current job. In the end, the possibility always exists that you'll stay. Don't shoot yourself in the foot by making co-workers suspicious and then maybe not landing a new job.

III. GATHERING GOOD REFERENCES

Many applicants are under the impression that employers no longer ask for references or that they never actually call them. Not so. Reference checking is a critical factor in hiring.

A reference check can reveal information—like lacking a college degree—that candidates omit or even lie about during interviews. A conversation with a reference can also shed light on an applicant's personality in a way that a résumé cannot. When an employer contacts references, he or she wants to know about the relationship with the applicant, if there were any problems that interfered with his or her performance, how the applicant handles difficult situations and if there is room for improvement.

An unfavorable reference check can even cost candidates a job that they thought was a guarantee. Employers can extend an offer letter and then revoke it if a reference check is not favorable.

Choose the right references

Picking the right references can be tricky if you don't know what to look for.

One common mistake is providing the name of someone who can only provide your dates of employment and job title, and nothing else. You don't want to leave the hiring manager feeling as though you're wasting his or her time by providing useless references who don't know much about you.

Your goal should be to pick references who will distinguish you from the other candidates interviewing for the position.

Make sure your references are ready and willing

Before you start giving out names and contact information, you should call the people on your list. Ask if they are willing to be a reference and make sure you're both on the same page about your work history and even your personal relationship.

For example, maybe you thought your last boss found your sense of humor hilarious, but really he thought you didn't take your job seriously. You also want to make sure your reference remembers you clearly—if not, you don't want the hiring manager finding this out before you.

Make sure your references are prepared

To avoid a reference passing along potentially unfavorable information, prep your reference thoroughly before you share the name with the hiring manager. By telling your reference about the position requirements and then asking how they see you adding value to the organization, you should get a very good feel for how the reference will respond.

Being sneaky doesn't work

Sometimes a hiring manager doesn't have to pick up the phone to see some warning signs of a bad applicant. If a candidate has no supervisors as references from any positions, it is indeed a big red flag, as are incorrect phone numbers, only cell phone numbers and names without job titles. If you're tempted to use a friend's cell phone as "the company HR department," think again.

Companies have gotten wise to candidates who list inaccurate contact numbers on their reference lists, and can find the HR department's number themselves and verify the information.

Reference checks benefit you, too

In addition to basic, factual information, a reference can reassure an employer that the person is right for the job and provide tips on what kind of manager the applicant needs.

The thing to remember is that hiring managers are not out to get you; they want to learn more about you. Their goal is to hire the best candidate for the job, and that means somebody they want to work with every day. Good references can help you get not only the job, but also a boss and co-workers that you like.

Building your reference list

It is never too early to begin preparing for the day when you will need an employment reference. Here's what you should be doing from Day One to ensure you have access to quality references when you need them:

MAINTAIN CONTACT WITH KEY BUSINESS ASSOCIATES. Janice, a former systems engineer, developed many professional relationships in her two-year stint at her former Internet company before it went bankrupt. Shortly after her company closed its doors, she started a networking group made up of her former colleagues from various companies. Together, they built a network of contacts that assisted each of them in landing their next jobs.

BUILD PERSONAL RELATIONSHIPS WITH CO-WORKERS WHEN YOU KNOW THE END IS NEAR. In addition to being personally fulfilling, personal relationships with former co-workers can often be the foundation of a strong and valuable network. People who are recently unemployed usually have a wealth of contacts from their job that should be tapped into while still fresh in their minds. Help your co-worker explore his or her network and both of you could reap the rewards. Think of it as double-dipping. Through your personal relationship, both you and your friend have each doubled the number of people with whom you can network.

BEFORE LEAVING A JOB, ALWAYS ASK SEVERAL OF YOUR TRUSTED COLLEAGUES IF THEY WILL SERVE AS YOUR REFERENCES. If they will, ask for their personal contact information and use it to get in touch from time to time. Julie was on the senior management team of the company where she worked before it filed for bankruptcy and was acquired by one of its competitors. By staying in touch with some of her fellow executives—including the CEO—she was able to build a consulting business of her own by securing their business as they landed new jobs.

If your best efforts to stay in touch have been unsuccessful, don't despair. There are many ways to locate a missing colleague. Here are several:

- Search the Internet using a directory assistance service.

- Use an Internet search engine to search by your colleague's name.

- Dig deep into the social networking sites you belong to.

- Check the phone book in the community in which your colleague may reside.

- Check the university that your former colleague attended to find out if they have an alumni association that may help you get back in touch.

- Many large companies that go out of business or have had massive layoffs have alumni sites that help their employees stay in touch. Search the Internet and you just may find one for your former employer.

- When a company files for bankruptcy, its assets are often acquired by another company. Personnel records may have been forwarded to one of the companies that acquired your former company's assets. Track down who bought what and you may find that missing link.

- Be proactive. Do your own background check with an online product like SureCheck.

If all of these efforts fail and you still don't have a reference, it may be time to switch gears. If you've done any freelance work, one of your clients would make a perfect reference. Do you do any volunteer work? Do you sit on any boards? If so, the people with whom you work on these volunteer assignments can likely attest to your work ethic, skills and professional abilities. Just remember to ask their permission before giving out any of their personal contact information.

IV. QUITTING WITHOUT BURNING BRIDGES

In December 2006, British worker Steve Moseley bought a lottery scratch card and discovered he'd won £1 million. He immediately told his boss to "stick it" and threw all the money he had on him at his colleagues. "Twenty minutes later he realized he hadn't won and then asked for his job back," his boss told the BBC. "I was a bit reluctant, but I gave it to him after making him ask a few times." A few days later, he reportedly resigned after unending teasing by his co-workers.

The lesson: You never know what's going to happen next, so don't be so quick to burn your bridges.

The world is much smaller than we sometimes think. You never know when or how paths will cross again, especially considering the fluidity of today's job market. When you're leaving a job, it's not the time to burn bridges, no matter how tempting it might be. Years down the road, you never know who will be interviewing you for that job you're dying for or who will be hired to sit in the cube next to you.

Whether leaving by choice or not, here are some dos and don'ts to consider before you tell your boss to stick it:

DO use professionalism and courtesy in announcing your intention to leave the company. Advise your direct supervisor first. Then tell colleagues and department staff.

DON'T do it at the last minute. Give your employer advance notice so there is enough time to arrange for your successor. Generally, acceptable notice is two to four weeks. Work with your current and future employers to set a time frame that works for both them and you.

DO write a professional letter of resignation. No need for lengthy explanations, you can simply state that you are resigning from your position to pursue other interests or opportunities. Whether you loved or hated your job or your supervisor, the outcome should be the same: a brief, respectful letter stating your intention to leave.

DON'T bad-mouth the company. Once others know you are leaving, naysayers may seek you out to share their feelings of discontent.

If you want to leave on good terms, don't be associated with disgruntled or unhappy employees.

DO finish the job. Don't leave projects half-completed. Provide a list of projects and review what can or needs to be completed before you depart. Don't disappear. Avoid short-timer's attitude. Stay an active and contributing member of your team during your last days at work. Work hard and do your best to leave a good and lasting impression.

DON'T leave your desk or office in disarray. Take a day to organize your materials for your successor. Leave the company assets behind. Unless you brought something from home or paid for that stapler with your own money, it should stay on your desk.

DO offer to train your replacement if time permits. If you leave before that person comes on board, make yourself available to answer questions in person or over the phone.

DON'T send boastful or sobbing farewell e-mails. If you choose to use e-mail to notify colleagues that you are leaving, provide your contact information—these people are part of your network.

DO use your exit interview time wisely. Regardless of what you are told, this is not the time to trash your boss or your boss's boss. If you haven't discussed your concerns about a co-worker in the past, don't use this as an opportunity to reveal them for the first time. If you have voiced concern, however, this is the time to reiterate it professionally. Remember: Leaving with class and grace will never come back to haunt you. Exiting on a sour note can.

How to resign the right way . . .

Jack Anderson
928 W. Irving Road
Des Moines, IA 50301

June 2, 2008
Randall King
President
King Marketing, Inc.
200 N. Polk Street
Des Moines, IA 50303

Randall,

I'll be stepping down from my position as senior account director effective June 16th. I've been offered an executive position in the marketing department of a large nonprofit organization. As you're aware, I began my career in nonprofit and have been itching to get back as I round out my career.

Thank you for your continued confidence in my work over the past nine years; I appreciate all you've done for me. You've provided me with many growth opportunities and I've learned a lot while working with you.

If you hire a replacement while I'm still here, I'd be more than happy to help train him/her. If not, I'll provide you with my contact information so I can answer any questions by e-mail or telephone.

It's been a pleasure working with you, Randall.

Sincerely,

Jack Anderson

And how to resign the wrong way . . .

Jack Anderson
928 W. Irving Road
Des Moines, IA 50301

June 2, 2008

Randall King
President
King Marketing, Inc.
200 N. Polk Street
Des Moines, IA 50303

Hey Randy,

I know we've worked together for a long time, but it's time for me to move on to greener pastures. I've been in this dead-end job long enough, don't ya think? I accepted a new gig at the top of the food chain for a nonprofit. I know what you're thinking, but I gotta tell ya, it pays a heck of a lot more than I'm getting here.

Well, buddy, I appreciate all the help you've given to me over the years. I also appreciate the numerous free happy hours, company dinners and posh hotels you've put me up in. I can't forget all of the "business trips" I've been able to take on the company dime, either. You're a generous guy, Rand.

My last day will be tomorrow. Sorry for the short notice, but I'm kind of anxious to blow this popsicle stand.

It's been real.

PEACE!
Jack

Chapter 15

GETTING THE AX

I. SIGNS YOUR JOB IS IN DANGER

Think a pink slip could be headed in your direction? Most people who are let go know their time is up or (in retrospect) say they should have seen it coming. While there are no sure signs of professional apocalypse, here are some clues your job may be in peril:

You're out of the loop

You no longer get advanced notice of company news or reports; and you seem to be losing your voice in organizational matters. You are not copied on memos you normally receive, or invited to meetings you usually attend.

Your boss has an eye on you

You feel as if you're being scrutinized more closely and that your boss no longer trusts you. Your decisions are constantly questioned, your expense reports are put under a microscope and you have less latitude to work independently.

You're getting the Siberia treatment

You used to know all the scoop—be it business or social in nature. Now your co-workers avoid you and the last conversation you had with your superiors was a lame attempt at pleasant banter.

You had a bad review

You received a poor performance rating and a disproportionate amount of negative feedback. If you received a warning or were given a "performance improvement plan," it's really time to start packing!

Your superior is leaving paper trails

Your boss communicates with you predominately in writing. You receive memos pointing out errors, criticizing your performance and confirming any meetings or discussions the two of you have had.

You and your boss are not getting along

Corporate management will swear it's not personal, yet many down-sizings are actually ways to get rid of unpopular or "blacklisted" employees. Performance is a subjective judgment and managers are more likely to get rid of people they don't like.

Your mentor is gone

The executive who always championed you has left the company or been rendered powerless.

TRUE TALES OF FIRINGS GONE GOOD: CLASHING VALUES

I was fired from a job about ten years ago, and it was the best thing that could have happened to me at the time—although I didn't know it then. I had been looking for a new job when I "resigned," but was hanging on to the one I had for health insurance purposes. My reason for being fired and the agency owner's reason for jostling me toward the door are likely different, if asked. I received the line about "going in a different direction," when in fact, he had downsized my role a few weeks prior. (I went crazy pretending to be busy—it wasn't fun!) The bottom line is that I realized that my values and style were much different from his, and I wasn't going to change what I believed to be right. . . . Today I represent wonderful clients as a publicist. What my clients see, hear and experience is what they get. They get the real me, not someone who spins words. For that I am proud!

— Gail S., Milwaukee, Wisc.

You publicly messed up

You made a blatant error that embarrassed your boss or made the company look bad. Or, you're part of a team that goofed up and they need a scapegoat.

New blood has taken over

Your company is about to merge, be acquired or undergo reorganization and your leader suddenly disappears. New hires have become the wave of the future and they've been given the directive to "shake things up."

You're being set up to fail

You've been assigned to an undesirable territory or given impossible tasks with unrealistic deadlines and little support.

You've been stripped of your duties

You've been asked to compile a report of all your ongoing projects and pushed hard to finish one or two specific projects. Or, you've been relieved of your core duties so that you can work on meaningless "special projects." You are encouraged not to do your usual long-term planning.

You're hearing rumors

If you're hearing rumors of your demise, take heed: Where there's smoke, there's fire!

At one point or another we're all vulnerable to the proverbial corporate ax. Don't live in denial. If you recognize more than one of these signs, it's time to look for greener pastures and take steps to reverse your fate.

TRUE TALES OF FIRINGS GONE GOOD: DOT-COM BUST

I got fired from a dot-com and it led me to go into business for myself and take the first real vacation I had since high school (35 years ago), and got me eventually to a nonprofit library/ museum, which I really enjoy. It also led to me getting a bimonthly history of science column, which is beginning its fifth year. By the way, that dot-com showed me there is no upper limit on how fast people can spend someone else's money.

— Neil G., Philadelphia, Penn.

II. DON'T WAIT AND SEE

With the emotional, financial and social strains a job loss causes, nobody is ever fully prepared. But you can make sure you're well set if the worst happens. You plan for everything else, why not a layoff? If you're sensing any of the warning signs we've mentioned, or if you just have a feeling the corporate wind is shifting, it's always best to be prepared.

Keep records

Have copies of everything that is important to you and keep a copy of it at home, away from the office. In a layoff or firing situation, a company will likely block your network and e-mail access while you're getting the news. Respect proprietary and confidential information, but otherwise make copies of any projects, letters, referrals, numbers, figures and statistics you might need to show examples of your work and build your portfolio. Make sure you have copies of personal files, performance appraisals and reviews.

Make a duplicate of your Rolodex and e-mail address book

Contacts may be more important than skills in some careers. Backup all your contacts, databases and important lists—these could be key in finding your next job or gathering references. This includes client and contact names, addresses, e-mail addresses and phone numbers. Keep a hard and digital copy.

Take inventory

Do a mental inventory of your career. Look at your accomplishments, qualifications and transferable skills. Determine what your next steps might be and whether you would stay in that profession, seek out a competitor, etc.

Reach out to your network

Touch base with clients, people you have met at trade shows and through professional associations, even competitors. It can be as simple as a phone call or e-mail message. This will keep your name fresh in their minds when job opportunities come their way. Use it to line up your referrals, too.

Start to get your support system in place

Who can you rely on in hard times? You may need emotional or spiritual support, advice and counsel, or even financial support should it come to that. Give a heads-up to people who can help you if you need it—this way it won't be coming completely out of the blue.

Visit your doctor

One of the most stressful parts of losing a job is the loss of health-care benefits. If you suspect a layoff, take care of medical needs while you still have insurance.

Act fast

If your company announces layoffs or says jobs may be cut in the future, act now. Don't wait to see what happens down the road or if it will affect you. This way you'll be ready if you're asked to leave.

Always save samples of your work

In the course of your career, it's easy to let the day-to-day duties of your job get in the way of planning for the future. Don't make this mistake. Keeping samples of your work will enable you to write a quality résumé or update the one you already have. In addition, these materials will come in handy if one day you need to assemble a portfolio of your work. Career experts suggest that you keep your samples in a file at your home. They warn against keeping this file at your office in the event you are asked to leave your job suddenly and are unable to take your files with you.

TRUE TALES OF FIRINGS GONE GOOD: LESSONS LEARNED

I am an extremely successful immigration lawyer at the age of 56. I was fired quite a few times in my life. Looking back, they all happened for very great reasons. When I first came to America, I could not speak English well, but I needed money. I went looking for jobs. In the late '60s, Chicago did not allow waitresses to serve drinks under the age of 21. I lied and said I was 21 in order to land the job. I was 19 at the time and did not know the difference between a martini and a Manhattan. Yet I eventually became the head waitress at a vegetarian hotel in Catskills, N.Y., after going through several jobs. After I graduated law school in 1976, I found it extremely difficult to find a good job. There were no, or very few, Asians practicing law, let alone Asian *women* practicing law. I was fired many times, but each time I learned something. My former bosses and I remain good friends. And now, I have built an extremely successful law firm with some great people. Being fired is not the worst experience. Usually there is a good reason; even though I know it is non-kosher to say this, God or our destiny demands it to help us mature. Every setback is an opportunity to gain and to learn.

— Margaret W., Cleveland, Ohio

III. HOW TO GET FIRED

Want to guarantee your spot in the unemployment line? Try some of these moves.

1: Don't bother learning what's expected of you

Sit down with your manager and make sure you understand exactly what your job entails, your deadlines and any relevant department policies. This eliminates ambiguity and ensures you'll know how your performance measures up.

2: Learn to say, "That's not part of my job description," and use it frequently

Everyone needs to set limits, but doing only the bare minimum sends a clear message that you're just interested in a regular paycheck. Sooner or later, your boss will start looking for someone willing to take more initiative.

3: Go shopping in the supply closet

While you're at it, run a few errands with the company car and pad your expense report. Stealing from the company is one of the best ways to guarantee your immediate dismissal.

4: Treat deadlines more like guidelines

When you procrastinate, everyone suffers. Your missed deadlines reflect poorly on you and your boss, and they delay everyone else on the project, since they can't finish their work until you do yours.

5: Consistently work "abbreviated" workdays

Want to show your boss how little you care about your job or career progress? Regularly come in late and leave early. After all, if you can't be trusted to show up on time, how can your boss trust you with more responsibility?

6: Bring your personal life to work

It's inevitable that personal business is going to pop up during work hours. But keep in mind that cubicles don't lend any privacy, so the whole office can hear—and be distracted by—you making that appointment with your facialist. Keep personal calls and errands to a minimum during work hours.

7: Forget teamwork—look out for No. 1

No one wants to work with an arrogant employee who steals ideas or an egotistical worker who demeans others. Helping your coworkers doesn't make you a pushover, it makes you smart. Likeable employees move up the company ranks more quickly, and your colleagues will be more likely to help you find leads when you launch your next job search.

8: Complain about your job to anyone who will listen

Whether your pay is too low, the work is drudgery or you think your boss is an idiot, be careful of who hears you complain. If it gets back to your boss, she may just put you out of your misery.

TRUE TALES OF FIRINGS GONE GOOD: ETHICAL DECISION

Back in 1978, I got fired from a job reading manuscripts for a well-known literary agent—who turned out to be a crook. I had serious ethical problems with the way this company was run—to the point where I took my evidence and met with a representative from the New York state attorney general's office. Customers were being misled to the point of fraud, and workers were treated with near-sweatshop conditions. I began job hunting within about a week of landing the job, once I realized what was going on—and began to investigate changing the conditions (e.g., starting a union). It didn't take long for upper management to start perceiving me as a troublemaker; I was fired after five months. . . . I am not at all sorry that I didn't stay with the crooked company, even though it led to even leaner times. Eventually, I pulled through and began building my own *ethical* business.

— Shel H., Hadley, Mass.

IV. SO YOU WERE FIRED

It can happen to anyone at anytime. A softened economy forces your employer to make cuts; your company merges with another and staffing changes; your department is restructured; a new boss cleans house; or you simply didn't perform to your manager's expectations. Whatever the reason, anytime is now. Here's what you can do to stay afloat:

Q: Is it better to pre-empt a firing by resigning instead?

A: In most cases, no. Out of pride, many people fall into this trap and wind up waiving claim to severance pay, benefits, earned bonuses and commissions and unemployment compensation. With so many victims of downsizings and reorganizations, being "let go" doesn't carry the stigma it once did—in fact most prospective employers won't even bat an eye!

Q: Should I try to negotiate a better severance package?

A: By all means, yes. According to the National Employee Rights Institute (NERI), employees have more bargaining power than they realize. Don't be pressured into signing anything on the spot. Tell your employer you need to review the proposed agreement with your legal and financial advisers. Then, check the company policy manual to find out what is standard practice for employees in your situation. If you can, talk to others whom the company has terminated. You can argue your case on merits such as length of service, specific accomplishments and amount of time required to find comparable employment in today's labor market. Be sure to document your achievements, and if your family has special needs (due to illness or disability) you may want to let your company know the hardships this termination may cause.

Remember, money is not the only thing at stake. Consider how long you will continue to be covered under company health and life insurance and the status of any earned—or close to being earned—bonuses, commissions, vacation time and vesting in 401(k), pension and profit sharing accounts. You also may want outplacement services or an agreed-upon letter of reference. Also think about getting your severance payment as salary continuation rather than a lump sum agreement. Salary continuation often allows for a continuation of disability benefits and also lets you answer yes when asked if you're still employed.

Q: What's the best course of action for finding a new job?

A: Take a day or so to process what has happened and vent to your spouse or best friend. Then, after shoring yourself up by reviewing your strengths and accomplishments, start calling people in your network who can be helpful to you, including former co-workers, suppliers and customers. Letting a colleague, vendor or client know that you'll no longer be working with them is not only a courtesy, but can prove a valuable source of leads. Then, work on your résumé and start an all-points attack that, in addition to networking, includes contacting recruiters, conducting industry research, cold-calling target companies and searching online job listings.

Q: How should I respond to those who ask why I left my last position?

A: Keep it brief. Be calm and objective; never assign blame. End your explanation on a positive note by emphasizing your main accomplishments and what the experience has taught you.

Q: How can I keep my spirits up?

A: Recognize that you will likely experience the five steps of dealing with loss: denial, anger, bargaining, depression and, finally, acceptance. Don't be too hard on yourself if you get down now and then. On the other hand, try not to dwell on anger or bitterness; instead channel that energy into your search. Take care of your physical and emotional health by exercising, eating well and surrounding yourself with positive and supportive people. And make sure you start each day with a plan. A sense of purpose and accomplishment will go a long way in making you feel better and landing you that new job.

TRUE TALES OF FIRINGS GONE GOOD: PRE-EMPTIVE MOVE

In anticipation of being fired, I quit a job once with no prospects of a replacement job lined up. I was working in the marketing department for a large international company that decided to reorganize and move the marketing function out of state. Having roots in New York I decided to stay and the company actually went out of the way to place me in accounting, which I thought was odd—being in marketing I was much better with words than with numbers. After several months I realized I was not suited for the job and decided to leave to "pursue other interests," which, in retrospect, was a good thing because I reinvented myself and used my marketing background to secure a public relations position with a leading Long Island agency. After several years I was running the agency and had an equity position in the firm, too. We have since sold the company and I have established an excellent reputation in public relations and found a career that I am well-suited to.

— Don M., Rockville Centre, N.Y.

Chapter 16

MOVING ON

Regardless if you made up your mind to quit, already left on your own accord or were fired, you're free. If you've listened to us, you have great references, an impressive résumé and flawless interview skills—you are more than prepared to jump into another job search. It's time to get you started on the next chapter of your career.

I. CERTIFIED JOB-HOPPER? PROS AND CONS OF JUMPING FROM JOB TO JOB

When baby boomers entered the work force more than half a century ago, they found a job and stayed put. In fact, many boomers still hold their first jobs today, and plan to keep them until retirement. On the other hand, Generation X and Y workers will tell you they've held five jobs since their college graduations. They're anxious to get their feet wet in different arenas, scaling the ranks of as many companies as possible until they reach the top.

> **BY THE NUMBERS: JOB-HOPPING**
> People in their twenties change jobs every eighteen months and one-third of our work force switches jobs every year, according to the Bureau of Labor Statistics. Additionally, the average American will have held an average of ten jobs between the ages of 18 and 38.

Frequent job changes, also known as "job-hopping," might make you look like an unstable employee to employers. Companies would rather hire someone who's stayed in a job for a long time. It shows you have loyalty and most likely, you'd stay with their organization for a long time, too. At the same time, you don't want to get left in the dust.

The reality is that after two or three years, most people need to reevaluate their work situation.

- Are you still learning?

- Are you still challenged?

- Is there room for you to move up?

- If you're stuck in a career standstill after a short period of time, why shouldn't you switch trades to somewhere that you can grow?

So, is job-hopping a crippling career move? Let's take a moment to evaluate the pros and cons.

Pro: Figuring out what you like

You'll never know what you like—or what you're good at—until you try it. Job-hopping allows you to discover where you like to work (at home or an office?), how you like to work (micro-managed or as a free sprit?) and what sector you prefer (corporate or nonprofit?).

Con: Landing in a worse position

If you're unhappy and bored in your current position, it's natural to look for something new. Just be careful; the last thing you want is to take the first opportunity that comes your way, just for the sake of getting out. You could end up worse off than when you started.

Pro: Making more money

Generally speaking, when you make a career change, it's usually onto greener pastures (pun intended). That being said, you can usually expect more money (or at least the same amount) when you switch positions.

Con: Explaining yourself

If your résumé shows that you've held three jobs in the past year, you have some explaining to do. If you worked for three different companies that didn't provide any opportunities for advancement, that's one thing; if you didn't like the coffee they served, it's another.

The trick to job-hopping is being able to showcase the contributions you made while you were there. You might have only been with an organization for one year but if in that time you increased sales by 110 percent and doubled the clientele, it will show more about your work ethic and less about the job duration.

Pro: Building your network

The more jobs you work, the more people you meet. The more people you meet, the more contacts you make. The more contacts you make, the bigger your network becomes. The bigger your network is, the better job opportunities you'll have. Comprende?

Con: Moving too fast

It's easy to be hungry for more when you're in a stagnant career. Unfortunately, some things—like moving up in the company—take time. If you leave your job before you're given the opportunity to advance, you're selling yourself short.

Pro: Learning new skills

Each time you change positions or work environments, you open yourself up to a learning opportunity. Job-hopping will help you build your skill set, making you a more marketable employee in the long run.

Overall, it's important to plan carefully and take each opportunity seriously. Let's get one thing straight: If you're leaving your jobs for frivolous reasons—like you want your own office or you don't get free office supplies—you won't get far in your hunt for engaging work. But if you're hopping for the right reasons, you can find yourself in a rewarding situation—for you and your employer.

II. ARE YOU EMPLOYABLE?

For some people, "If it ain't broke, don't fix it" is a guiding principle. And if you've found one job, you can certainly find another. You know all you need to know about job hunting, right?

If you find your job hunt isn't giving you anything but a stress headache, maybe it's time for a refresher. Ask yourself these questions:

Is my résumé targeted?

Just because you're applying for multiple jobs, don't assume the same résumé works for every position. Each job posting will stress different qualities over others, so rework each résumé to highlight the experience and skills that correspond to that particular employer. Your résumé will prove not only that you're qualified for the job but that you also pay attention to detail.

Am I networking?

We've said it once; we'll say it again—networking is crucial. Think about this: There is only one of you and there are thousands of job openings. The more people know you're looking for a job, the better your chances of finding one are. You can never be sure who will know of an available position. Networking can also connect you to a hiring manager, directly or indirectly, giving you the edge over other candidates.

Do I know something about the companies I'm applying to?

"Tell me what you know about the company" or "Why would you fit in well here?" have become staple interview questions, so don't be caught off guard. Shrugging your shoulders and saying, "I don't know" isn't going to score you points. Look at the company's Web site and read press releases and newspaper articles to see what's going on with your prospective future boss. In addition to preparing for the interview, you'll learn whether the company and its culture are a right fit for you.

Am I targeting my job search?

Sending out several résumés is key to finding a job, but you also need to be selective about the jobs to which you're applying. While you don't need to possess every single skill listed on a posting, you should at least be qualified for the position and prove that you have transferable skills. Your targeted résumé will help prove you're a serious candidate and have the right qualifications for the position.

If you're spending time applying for jobs you're not qualified for, you're wasting valuable time you could be devoting to a position that's a better fit. If you recognize where your strengths lie and what transferable skills you possess, you'll see better results than if you apply to any posting you come across.

Has someone else evaluated my résumé and interview technique?

Feedback is critical to job hunting. Ask someone else to read your résumé and review it as if they were hiring for the job. Friends or colleagues can provide objective points of view to help you revise your résumé.

Your interview skills need the same attention. Are your answers succinct or too short? Thorough or rambling? What you think you're saying isn't necessarily what others hear, so find this out now rather than in the interview. If you don't think that a colleague or friend can offer constructive feedback, make an appointment with an interview coach.

How am I presenting myself?

Employers are assessing your presentation before you even show up for an interview.

Your e-mails and phone conversations with hiring managers or recruiters should also send a professional message. Don't send e-mails written in all capital letters and/or using three exclamation points—it's bad netiquette in personal correspondence, but it's even worse in business.

Put the same thought into your outgoing voice mail message. Don't try to be funny by playing 30 seconds of your favorite song or talking with a mouthful of food. Hiring managers might hang up instead of ask you to call them back. Give a normal, casual greeting, or use one of the preprogrammed options that come with most accounts.

If a recruiter calls you, don't try to hold a conversation with your TV blaring in the background or your child screaming on your lap. If you're asked whether it's a good time to talk, you can be honest and say you're in the middle of something. Then ask if he or she can call you back in 15 minutes or find another day that's convenient for both of you. You'll be prepared to answer all the recruiter's questions and won't be distracted.

Your goal is to find a better job than you had, right? So you have to conduct a better search this time around. Put the effort in and you'll see the results.

III. TAKING THE FREELANCING ROUTE

Now that you've been released from the chains of your old job, perhaps the direction you want to take is into freelancing and contract work. No more of the nine-to-five grind! No more answering to The Man. From now on, YOU are The Man.

Being a free agent is exciting, rewarding and gives you carte blanche to choose your own hours and assignments. But standing out from the estimated 10 million independent contractors in the United States can be a challenge.

Some workers freelance while they look for a traditional full-time job, but most are freelancing because they've made a conscious lifestyle choice. They want to better balance and integrate their lives and work and be able to control what they do, how many hours they work and how much money they make.

Employers are inclined to hire freelancers and contractors, too, because it provides more latitude to conduct their operations. In fact, 55 percent of employers told CareerBuilder.com they have either relied on freelance workers and contractors or intend to in the future.

Employers can hire based on specific skill sets for individual projects and outsource more operations, ranging from design and marketing to IT. This allows businesses to easily augment or reduce staff levels based on workflow and control costs by dialing up or down payroll and minimizing benefits coverage.

If you're seeking the flexibility and autonomy of freelancing, here's how to build your client base and fatten your wallet:

Specialize in a growing niche

Examine your skills and background to identify the unique services and value you can offer. Then think of ways to apply them in an area that has high and growing demand—and not a lot of experts to do the work. For example, freelance writer Mary L. was having little luck finding travel and entertainment assignments, but after taking inventory of past projects, found several pieces she wrote for her former employer's IT department. Today, she has a flourishing technical writing practice and more work than she can handle.

Nurture your network

Stay top-of-mind by regularly keeping in touch with your network. Go where the people who can hire you are—attend the same conferences, join the same associations and read the same magazines and newsletters. Call your friends and colleagues and tell them what you are looking for and what you have to offer. Be sure to contact former bosses and co-workers, too. If you left the company on good terms, this can be an excellent way to get clients.

Join a service

There are many Web sites, like Sologig.com, that connect independent contractors and employers. Unlike many freelance sites, Sologig.com is not a bidding platform. Job seekers are not required to register or log on to the site, and do not pay to post a profile or apply to projects. Instead, employers purchase project postings and access to the 1.1 million profiles and résumés in Sologig.com's database.

Build referrals

Referrals are one of the easiest and most effective ways to build your business. And, once you get rolling, they have a snowball effect. To encourage referrals, first be sure to take care of your existing customers in a way that will leave them absolutely thrilled with your services. When the kudos come in, ask for testimonials and referrals. One independent accountant even began his own "referral reward" program, where he sends a thank-you note along with a $25 gift certificate to those who send new clients to him.

Subcontracting

Subcontract your services out to other firms or independent professionals in your field. For example, a freelance graphic designer supplements her direct business by subcontracting with a large ad agency that uses her talent when it has more work than it can handle or can't do the task as efficiently or economically. The designer works behind the scenes and is paid by the agency—often at a lower rate than if she got the project on her own. It's a win-win for both the designer and the agency and has been a great way to build the designer's portfolio.

More is good

The more qualified prospects you reach, the more clients you will have. Even if you can only handle several assignments at a time, a larger client base gives you the option of choosing the most exciting and rewarding projects. And isn't that why you became a free agent in the first place?

Establish yourself as an expert

Becoming known as an expert can be some of the best advertising you can get. Write articles in industry magazines, newsletters and trade journals and arrange to speak at professional or trade association conferences on topics related to your niche. Those who like your articles and speeches will contact you when they want more information, some may even become clients. Post your articles and speeches on your Web site, send "FYI" copies to your clients and associates and include them in your marketing literature.

POP QUIZ: What are employers willing to pay contractors and freelancers?

A) $50 an hour
B) $75 per hour
C) $100 per hour
D) All of the above

ANSWER: D. Employers are willing to pay top dollar for skilled freelancers and contractors. One-in-ten would pay $100 or more per hour; nearly one-in-five would pay $75 or more per hour; and 34 percent would pay $50 or more per hour.

IV. WHAT JOB IS RIGHT FOR YOU?

Are you an introvert or an extrovert? Are you structured or free-wheeling?

Your personality really can determine whether you merely survive in your position or thrive in your career. While there is no good or bad personality type, there are certain jobs that suit one personality better than another.

Often personality traits are revealed as particular strengths and weaknesses in job performance. For instance, quieter, more introverted people may not do well in a position that requires delivering frequent presentations to senior management or a packed seminar hall.

Below is a list of common personality traits and examples of jobs that may fit well with those traits. Do you see yourself? Does your current career match with the suggested vocations? Are you:

LOGICAL, FACTUAL, ORGANIZED—These traits make management, accounting, electrician, computer programming or technical writing careers a good fit.

SENSITIVE, INTUITIVE, HANDS ON—Look to counseling, ministry, nursing or teaching.

ENTHUSIASTIC, OUTSPOKEN, AMBITIOUS—A career in TV, radio or advertising may suit you.

OPTIMISTIC, INQUISITIVE, FULL OF ENERGY—You may need a dynamic career to keep you interested, such as a tour guide or a sales position with extensive travel.

PRECISE, DETAIL-ORIENTED, ANALYTICAL, NEAT—Research, statistics or investigation may keep your mind occupied.

GREGARIOUS, INDEPENDENT, BORN TO LEAD—You may be drawn to power positions, such as a CEO, editor or government official.

IMAGINATIVE, DRAMATIC, PHILOSOPHICAL—Positions in psychology, drama, painting or music could hold your interest.

NURTURING, HUMANITARIAN, PROGRESSIVE—Consider a vocation in social work, philanthropy or a judicial career to foster your need to help people.

CREATIVE, SPONTANEOUS, INSIGHTFUL—Graphic arts, photography or working as a chef might help keep those creative juices flowing.

While this list may oversimplify the complex issues of personality profiling for employment, there is a burgeoning industry of personality profilers who are hired by both employers and individuals to help assess a person's chances of success in a particular job.

V. CHANGING CAREERS

In your quest for the "perfect job" how much of a change are you looking for? When you think about your last job, what comes to mind? Do you get the sense that your career is not the right fit for you? If you're feeling frustrated, unchallenged and unfulfilled in your work, the time might be right for you to make a major change.

Changing professions, however, is not something to do without some serious thought and consideration. Here are some guidelines to help you weigh your options and make a decision.

Job change vs. career change?

What is it that's really making you unhappy? Is it your supervisor or co-workers, the salary or company culture? Or is it something deeper? If you simply want to get away from a dysfunctional work environment or want a fatter paycheck, then you're probably seeking a simple job change. But if you are not finding fulfillment or contentment in the actual work you do, that's a sign to make a complete change.

Pinpoint your abilities

What are the things that come naturally to you? Do you find it easy to persuade others? Do you have a flair for working with numbers? Do you communicate better through the written word than you do in person? Think of your personal traits and use them to steer you to your new career.

Highlight your transferable skills

Transferable skills are the talents and experiences that can be utilized in many different careers and are not those things that are industry-specific. For example, if you have managerial experience, this is something that is useful in any industry. The same goes for communications savvy, computer know-how, writing proficiency, sales knack and event planning. It's all in the way you present these skills.

Learn what's needed

Are you willing to do what it takes to make the change? For example, someone interested in social work or nursing will likely need to pursue further education to be qualified. Entering a new industry might mean you need certification or a license. Make sure you are prepared to take these steps.

Be a detective

Do your research. Set up informational interviews with people in the career you desire. Ask them questions and request their candor. Find out if the industry is growing or declining. Learn about emerging opportunities. Delve into the salaries—both entry level and long-term earning potential.

The most important thing in changing careers is turning to something that will play on your strengths and skills, satisfy your desires and suit your personality.

VI: A JOB FOR EVERY NEED

We know that every job is as varied as every job seeker. Here are some jobs that may fit your needs and wants. Here are jobs that:

Let you work from home

1. Administrative assistant
2. Advertising sales agent
3. Computer software engineer
4. Corporate event planner
5. Copy editor
6. Desktop publisher
7. Data entry clerk
8. Insurance underwriter
9. Market research analyst
10. Paralegal

Take you back to school

1. Teacher (preschool, kindergarten, elementary, middle and secondary)
2. School counselor
3. School nurse
4. Principal
5. Postsecondary teacher
6. Librarian
7. Coach

8. Special education teacher
9. Dean/administrator
10. Teacher assistant

Let you shop

1. Personal assistant
2. Fashion merchandiser
3. Interior designer
4. Sommelier
5. Buyer
6. Event coordinator
7. Food critic
8. Senior shopping concierge
9. Wardrobe assistant
10. Customer service evaluator (mystery shopper)

Let you eat

1. Sommelier
2. Event planner
3. Chef
4. Quality control technician
5. Food scientist
6. Caterer
7. Restaurant critic
8. Dietician
9. Server
10. Product promoter

Let you hit the road

1. Automobile tester
2. Race car driver
3. Pilot
4. Firefighter
5. Emergency medical technician (EMT)
6. Taxi driver
7. Valet (parking attendant)
8. Ocean lifeguard
9. Bike messenger
10. Delivery driver

Let you dress casually

1. Electrician
2. Rock critic
3. Gardener/landscaper
4. Chef
5. High school teacher
6. Film editor
7. Graphic designer
8. Accessory designer
9. Computer tech support/consultant
10. Restaurant manager

Let you work with animals

1. Animal caretaker
2. Marine biologist
3. Park manager
4. High school science teacher

5. Animal groomer
6. Veterinary pathologist
7. Animal welfare lawyer
8. Zoo director
9. Animal-assisted therapist
10. Animal behavioral trainer

Let you have weird hair

1. Barista
2. Cosmetologist
3. Massage therapist
4. Server
5. Copy editor
6. Theater worker
7. Software development engineer
8. Web designer
9. Instructor (at an art college)
10. Photographer
11. Chemist
12. Mascot (pro sports or theme parks)

Let you get outdoors

1. Real estate agent
2. Landscape architect
3. Construction worker
4. Organic farmer
5. Sports referee
6. Tour guide
7. Camp counselor
8. Tennis instructor

9. Botanist
10. Skydiving instructor

Will never disappear

1. Doctor
2. Teacher
3. Mortician
4. Waste disposal manager
5. Scientist
6. Tax collector
7. Barber
8. Soldier
9. Religious leader
10. Law enforcement officer
11. Farmer
12. Construction worker

Crank up the scare factor

1. Coroner
2. Ghost hunter
3. Mystery writer
4. Mortician
5. Witch doctor
6. Embalmer
7. Crime scene cleanup
8. Grave digger/cemetery worker
9. Obituary writer
10. Crematorium technician

Let you globetrot

1. Travel nurse
2. Flight attendant
3. Meeting event planner
4. Wine buyer
5. Photojournalist
6. Sales representative
7. Long-distance freight truck driver
8. Au pair/nanny
9. Translator/interpreter
10. Promotional marketer

Have flexible schedules

1. Corporate positions
2. Non-tenured post-secondary teacher
3. Temporary employment service
4. Hospitality clerk
5. Library assistant
6. Hairstylist and barber
7. Retail positions
8. Fitness instructor
9. Restaurant staff
10. Taxi driver or chauffeur

Are good for early birds

1. Morning news producer
2. Newspaper deliverer
3. Schoolteacher
4. Refuse and recyclable material collector
5. Postal Service mail carrier

Are good for night owls

1. Reporter
2. Bartender/bouncer
3. Pastry chef
4. Movie projectionist
5. Disc jockey

Are good for early birds *and* night owls

1. Nurse
2. Doctor
3. EMT/paramedic
4. Chef/cook
5. Server
6. Host(ess)
7. Barista
8. Dishwasher
9. Police officer
10. Firefighter
11. Transit or railroad operator
12. Truck, bus or taxi driver
13. Chauffeur
14. Hotel employee
15. Security guard
16. Helpline and technical support staff

Let your inner party animal out

1. Event planner
2. Bartender
3. Booking manager
4. DJ

5. Nightclub manager
6. Bouncer
7. Travel guide
8. Promotions manager
9. Talent scout
10. Publicist

Are top secret

1. FBI special agent
2. CIA operations officer
3. Secret service special agent
4. Nuclear engineer
5. Detective
6. National security agency language analyst
7. Psychiatrist
8. Biometric technology developer
9. Cryptanalyst
10. Awards-show auditor

Are for TV junkies

1. Animator
2. Camera operator
3. Broadcast captioner
4. Broadcast news reporter
5. Film/video editor for broadcast/TV
6. Executive producer
7. Promotions producer
8. Director
9. Staff writer
10. Casting director

May not require a lot of experience

1. Traffic technician
2. Human resources assistant
3. Bill and account collector
4. Refuse and recyclable materials collector
5. Library technician
6. Light delivery truck driver
7. Occupational therapist aide
8. Interviewer
9. Nursing aide or orderly
10. Funeral assistant

Are fit for fitness buffs

1. Coach
2. Fitness director/gym manager
3. Nutritionist/dietician
4. Personal trainer
5. Sports instructor
6. Physical therapist
7. Professional athlete
8. Recreation and activity coordinator
9. Sports reporter/writer
10. Umpire/referee

THE BOTTOM LINE

Transitioning from one job to another is one of the most stressful things a person can experience. We're not saying it's going to be easy. It will be demanding, time-consuming and sometimes tedious, but it will be worth the effort. And remember, you get out what you put in, so get to putting!

SO START BUILDING!

Consider this: An average American who works 39.2 hours a week, with two weeks vacation and working 40 years, will spend about 78,400 hours on the job. The Bureau of Labor Statistics reports median job tenure for men is 4.1 years and 3.9 years for women.

The bottom line: You are going to spend a lot of time at many different jobs. How are you going to make them work?

Your career evolution doesn't stop here. We've given you the tools, now you have to put them to work. Bon voyage. Adieu. Farewell. And good luck in all your professional endeavors.

ABOUT THE CONTRIBUTORS

KATE LORENZ is the advice editor for CareerBuilder.com and manages the editorial content for CareerBuilder.com and its partner sites in the United States, Canada, and the U.K. She researches and writes about job search strategy, career management, hiring trends and workplace issues. She previously contributed to the book *Cube Monkeys: A Handbook for Surviving the Office Jungle*.

RICHARD CASTELLINI is chief marketing officer of CareerBuilder.com's North American operations. He is an expert on worker attitudes, job seeker behavior and employment trends, which he has discussed on CNN, FOX, FOX Business, CNBC and NPR. He has an MBA from Northwestern University's Kellogg School of Management.

ROSEMARY HAEFNER is vice president of human resources at CareerBuilder.com. She is a recognized authority on recruitment trends and tactics, job seeker behavior, workplace issues, employee attitudes, pay issues, workload and stress. Rosemary, who has an MBA from Northwestern University's Kellogg School of Management, has appeared on CNN, FOX, FOX Business, CNBC and NPR.

BRENT RASMUSSEN is the president of CareerBuilder.com's North American operations. He is an expert in leadership skills, high-impact management, motivating teams, hot job markets, plans to change jobs and career progress. Brent has been seen on FOX, FOX Business and BusinessWeek TV and heard on CBS National Radio and AP Radio. He has an MBA from Northwestern University's Kellogg School of Management.

OTHER CAREERBUILDER.COM CONTRIBUTORS TO THIS BOOK: Rachel Zupek, Anthony Balderrama, Jennifer Grasz, Tanya Flynn and Michael Erwin.

INDEX